"I do not think I have ever read a boo
more eager to pass it on than this one—
ger to evangelize than this one. Like its
Better yet, it is faithful to Scripture while overflowing with that least
common gift, common sense. Read it, practice it, then buy some more
and pass them out."
D. A. Carson, Trinity Evangelical Divinity School

"A fresh and refreshing encouragement from a gifted evangelist. Mack
Stiles has lived out what he teaches, both in North America and in the
Middle East. His material has been field-tested in two completely different parts of the world! So the principles you find in this book will be
transcultural and applicable to believers seeking to bear witness to Christ
wherever they are located in the world."
Lindsay Brown, Lausanne Committee for World Evangelization

"Most of what we read about evangelism puts heavy emphasis on evangelistic methods—'how to' evangelism. When's the last time you read a
book that focused attention on the evangelists themselves—their hearts,
their minds, their lives and, most of all, their message? This is such a
book, and it's explosive. *Marks of the Messenger* challenges and encourages
us, and makes us laugh and weep along the way. Mack Stiles is the most
gifted evangelist I know. And this book is saturated with biblical truth
and personal wisdom."
Thabiti Anyabwile, First Baptist Church of Grand Cayman

"Perhaps no part of the Christian life and ministry is easier to neglect,
postpone or just plain ignore than evangelism. And this is why I love
reading books on evangelism by true practitioners and
consistently live out this burden. Mack Stiles is o
loves people who need the gospel. If you, like
gelism, I highly recommend Mack's book."
C. J. Mahaney, Sovereign Grace Ministries

MARKS *of the*

MESSENGER

Knowing, Living and Speaking the Gospel

J. MACK STILES

Foreword by MARK DEVER

IVP Books

An imprint of InterVarsity Press
Downers Grove, Illinois

InterVarsity Press
P.O. Box 1400, Downers Grove, IL 60515-1426
World Wide Web: www.ivpress.com
E-mail: email@ivpress.com

InterVarsity Press® is the book-publishing division of InterVarsity Christian Fellowship/USA®, a movement of students and faculty active on campus at hundreds of universities, colleges and schools of nursing in the United States of America, and a member movement of the International Fellowship of Evangelical Students. For information about local and regional activities, write Public Relations Dept., InterVarsity Christian Fellowship/USA, 6400 Schroeder Rd., P.O. Box 7895, Madison, WI 53707-7895, or visit the IVCF website at <www.intervarsity.org>.

All Scripture quotations, unless otherwise indicated, are taken from the Holy Bible, New International Version®. NIV®. *Copyright ©1973, 1978, 1984 by International Bible Society. Used by permission of Zondervan Publishing House. All rights reserved.*

Design: Cindy Kiple
Images: Man walking through fog: John Warden/Getty Images
Jesus walking: Peter Brutsch/iStockphoto

ISBN 978-0-8308-3350-4

Printed in the United States of America ∞

Library of Congress Cataloging-in-Publication Data

Stiles, J. Mack, 1956-
Marks of the messenger: knowing, living, and speaking the Gospel /
J. Mack Stiles; foreword by Mark Dever.
p. cm.
Includes bibliographical references.
ISBN 978-0-8308-3350-4 (pbk.: alk. paper)
1. Witness bearing (Christianity) 2. Evangelistic work. I. Title.
BV4520.S6748 2010
248'.5—dc22

                                                                    2010000184

P 25 24 23 22 21 20 19 18 17 16 15 14 13 12 11 10 9 8 7 6 5 4 3 2

Y 31 30 29 28 27 26 25 24 23 22 21 20 19 18 17 16 15 14 13 12 11

To

David and Kris Lawrence

Brian and Joanne Parks

Colaborers and lifelong friends

CONTENTS

FOREWORD

Books on evangelism are either discouraging or encouraging. Think about it.

Few topics are more discouraging when talked about vaguely and guilt-inducingly than evangelism. "How many people have you led to Christ? This week?" "Why didn't you share the gospel with that new guy at work?" "You can only share the gospel correctly if you do it like this." "If you really believed this . . ." Never mind. You get the idea.

And yet, few topics are more encouraging when talked about with biblical wisdom, practical insight and genuine excitement. Stories of evangelism done faithfully, accounts of people's conversions—these are conversations that kindle my affections for Christ and stoke my enthusiasm to share the good news about him with others.

But, I have to say honestly, most books on evangelism are more of the discouraging variety. This book is different.

Not only is this book one of those rare encouraging books on evangelism, but it is one of those even more rare *instructive* books on evangelism. Think Packer or Metzger, only with more transparent passion and punch.

This book is like its author. I've known Mack for over twenty years. And reading this book is a lot like listening to him talk—an enjoyable experience, where excitement and wisdom mingle freely. Lots of Bible. Lots of stories. Stories, it has to be said, that are right next door to incredible.

If you wonder if these stories could really be true, let me just add my witness to at least some of them—Mack has a memory like an elephant and lives life in vivid colors. For decades now, I've seen Mack do exactly the kind of stuff that he talks about on these pages.

Mack is one of those people—like Spurgeon or Hudson Taylor—to whom amazing things happen. Why do all of these things happen to him? That's a question that only God can certainly answer. Is it because he is so careful to note, to remember, to recount, and so to encourage Christians and bring God more glory? Mack remembers so many stories. He remembers stories about my life better than I do! And he uses the great acts of God in his own experience to illustrate biblical truths—truths that are important for us to be reminded of.

In this book, we are given biblical clarity on the gospel, with extraordinary experience in evangelism. The result is an instructive exposé, a warning about where too many of us are today, about how we've become fuzzy around the edges—and sometimes even near the core—of the gospel. In this book, Mack puts the evangel back in evangelism. If we read it praying for God's Spirit to help us apply its truths to our own evangelism, we may do the same.

Mark Dever, Senior Pastor, Capitol Hill Baptist Church, Washington, D.C.
Director, 9Marks.org

ACKNOWLEDGMENTS

I owe a special thanks to my family: Leeann, Tristan, David and Isaac—fountains of great joy. Thanks to those who believed in this project from the start: Issa, Nigel, Ray, Jyothi, Onsy and Biju. Many thanks to Ted Callahan and his late wife, Judi, and to Tom Dupree and his late wife, Clara. Thanks also to B. Ray, Juann and daughter Adella. Special thanks to United Christian Church of Dubai, especially the Friday Foundations Class, and John and Keri Folmar. Also, thanks to the great folk at Capitol Hill Baptist Church, to whom I own such great debts: the entire concept of healthy marks, for one. I'm grateful especially to Mark and Connie Dever, and Michael and Adrienne Lawrence. Ross and Kathy Durham have been a help over the years in pointing me to the centrality of the gospel. I'm grateful for Jim and Beth Reed and their friendship, love and support. I'm grateful for the entire MENA team, especially Jamil, Hussam, Shaher, Zaher and Ellie, who graciously put up with an American in their midst. And the entire FOCUS team who cheerfully picked up the slack when I was hidden away writing, especially Joanna, Nisin, Adrian and Sara. Words can't express my gratitude to Lindsay Brown and his endless vision for the kingdom. Thanks also to the Swiss ski team friends, especially Piers. And the folks at Quest, especially Pete and Jackie, John and Helen, and Billy. And, of course, thanks to faithful and longtime editor, Andy Le Peau. Many others to whom gratitude is due are quoted in this book.

Dubai
August 2009

1

ROGER'S QUESTION

Don't Peddle the Gospel

Years ago my boss, Roger, asked me, "Mack, who do you want to be?"

He could tell I bristled at the administration required by my overly administrative job. I think he actually meant "don't complain." But I took him more seriously than he intended. So a couple of months later, after mulling that question over in my head, I decided to quit that job, pack up the family and move to the Middle East.

Roger thought I'd lost my mind.

We spent a year in transition and preparation and then, just as we readied to depart, 9/11 happened.

Still, I banged the "For Sale" sign in the front yard of my house the next day, so convinced was I that this was the very opportunity for me to be who I was meant to be. To join in the call of Christ that was wild and free and wonderful. To live the gospel with love and boldness. To show the world that the church's response to the horrific events of 9/11 were not military, but missionary.

At least that's how it felt on 9/12.

The gut check happened when the house sold on 9/13. Second thoughts swirled through my mind. Were we really moving to the place those suicide bombers lived? Thankfully my wife, more unwavering than her husband, kept us focused and on track so that we, with our three sons, moved to Dubai a few short months later.

And it's been wonderful.

We discovered, once we got here, that the Middle East is made of hospitable and wonderful people, the vast majority of whom are as far away from suicide bombers as most people in America are from chainsaw murderers. It turns out, living the Christian faith in the Muslim world is in some ways easier than living out faith in a secular society. I have far more genuine opportunities to share the gospel than I did in the United States.

Yet still, I'm amazed at how true those naive and noble thoughts were in the front yard of my house in Kentucky. It truly has been a time to pursue who I was meant to be, to be shaped by the truth of the gospel of Christ.

WHO DOES JESUS WANT US TO BE?

So, I've often thought of Roger and his question. "Who do you want to be?" I've wondered why we don't ask Roger's question more. I've wondered why we usually ask the question "What do you want to do?" I'm not exactly sure why that is. Maybe it's because we're so busy "doing" that we don't think first. Maybe it's because we're raised on the idea that we can make ourselves whatever we want to be. Maybe it's because we find our identity in our accomplishments or our jobs. Maybe it's the outcome we fear—after all you could say, "Look at Mack. He started thinking through who he was meant to be and he ended up moving to the Middle East."

Well, for whatever reason, I'm convinced we don't ask Roger's question enough. And if we don't ask the question, we get into all kinds of problems in life's situations. This isn't new news; after all, didn't your mother tell you to "think before you act"?

It's especially critical to know who we are meant to be spiritually. To leave Roger's question unasked in our Christian life gets us into a whole host of spiritual problems.

"Christian . . . who do you want to be?"

Most Christians, me included, would respond, "I want to be more like Jesus."

But wait. It's too easy to jump from wanting to be more like Jesus to "What Would Jesus *Do.*" Before we jump, we should make sure we understand who Jesus would have us *be.*

Acting without a biblical understanding of who Jesus wants us to *be* is the reason so many become unhealthy in their spiritual lives, producing unhealthy disciples and unhealthy churches.

In the same way, to act without a biblical understanding of who Jesus wants us to be in evangelism produces unhealthy evangelists.

I find that most Christians want to be able to share their faith. But without coming to grips with some basic principles about who we are to be as evangelists, we can produce some unhealthy evangelism. So become a healthy evangelist by first asking, "Who do we want to be as people who share their faith?" And we must ask, "Who would Jesus have us be—period?" This is a bedrock question.

And the answer, in a nutshell: Jesus asks his followers to *be* people of faith. That is, we put our complete faith and trust in him in two important ways.

We are people of faith by first believing in Christ. His story comes to us through the message of the gospel. We'll speak more about the message of the gospel in the next chapter, but it's enough to say now that there's some confusion about the gospel, and we need to make sure we've got it right so that we can be who we are meant to be.

Second, we are people of faith by becoming faithful followers. We place our trust in the teachings of Jesus from the Bible.[1]

Then, springing out of faith in Christ's work and commitment to his teaching, we endeavor to live faithful lives. We define faithful living according to what Jesus and his apostles define as faithful living in the Bible. It's a striking thing that we cannot please God without faith (Hebrews 11:6). That means two people can be doing the exact same thing, but one is kingdom work and the other is from the pits of hell. They may look the same, but to God in the spiritual realms, the equation doesn't work without faith.

Notice this commitment to faithful living, to action, to doing—including evangelism—only comes after we have answered the question of who we are to be, that is, people of faith in Christ. To share faith means that we must have faith first.

Sadly, there are many who are busy with religious work who never nail that down. The world is filled with people who are not people of faith first—including Sunday school teachers, pastors and missionaries.

18

One of them was my wife. She actively shared her faith in her youth group. Then it dawned on her, while sharing about faith with another high school student, that she wasn't a person of faith herself. She had not been clear that being a Christian was not a matter of being active in church or Christian culture, but rather was a matter of putting her complete faith and trust in Christ. Fortunately, she took the time to reorder her life, think through who Jesus wanted her to be and place her faith in him. But many never do.

So why have people jumped to action, in this case evangelistic action, before being people of faith? Maybe it's because they can. We have not been watchful enough about the conditions of people's hearts before we ask them to act, because with the right method or program, the condition of a person's heart isn't that important. We have become pragmatists.

THE PROBLEM WITH PRAGMATISM

There are numerous obstacles to becoming healthy evangelists. But I'm convinced that the greatest obstacle to healthy evangelism is pragmatism: "doing evangelism" before we ever think who we are meant to be as evangelists. The result is an evangelism that is twisted and deformed.[2]

Success drives pragmatic evangelism. Pragmatic evangelism never asks the question "Who are we to be as an evangelist?" Pragmatic evangelism only asks the question "What works?"

Pragmatic evangelism is "doing" evangelism in a way that elevates success and method over anything else. It becomes the business of evangelism. This may look cool or uncool, it may look relevant or irrelevant, but regardless, when evangelism is untethered to who we are meant to be as people of faith, evangelistic practice eventually becomes twisted and deformed. It becomes programmatic rather than personal; it becomes success at any cost, even if the cost is manipulation or even unethical practice. And sadly, because success sells, it's often unquestioned in the Christian community.

Pragmatic evangelism is about promotion. It's rarely concerned about the integrity of the message, since it's more about style and method than substance and authenticity. Jesus regularly told his disciples not to talk about him. Part of the reason so many are baffled by this command is our pragmatic commitment to promotional evangelism. Jesus understood that in the disciples' desire to promote, they would promote the wrong things in the wrong way.

After Peter has made the stunning confession that Jesus was the son of the living God (Matthew 16:16), Jesus strictly warns them not to speak of him. Why? Though they knew a bit about who Jesus was, they didn't have the message right. So when Jesus begins to teach about his coming torture and crucifixion, Peter rebukes Jesus for such an awful idea, proving he didn't understand the message—and this only a moment after Peter has spoken rightly about Christ's true identity. Jesus rebukes Peter and says that his thoughts are the thoughts of men and of Satan, not of God. Peter may have been the first pragmatic evangelist, but not the last.

Do you see the similarity with us? We can speak beautifully about the glorious revelation of Jesus being the Christ, and in almost the same breath speak "Satanic verses" that deny the cross.

Pragmatic evangelism offers methods. Shelves of Christian

bookstores are filled with books on evangelistic methods—both personal methods and methods for church growth. When those methods are no longer successful, rebels ridicule yesteryear's method and offer more palatable and effective methods in their place, which is really not that different than marketing the same product in a new and better wrapper.

Pragmatic evangelism counts: converts, members, programs, but rarely counts faithfulness to the message or the faithfulness of the messenger.

As a result most people, when they consider evangelism, think of questions that lead people to some spiritual conclusion, or service programs that gain applause from the community, or a way to tailor church services to be more appealing. I'm not opposed to soup kitchens or jazz in the church foyer as long as we don't think these things are the same thing as evangelism. But they will become unhealthy evangelism if they build on an unhealthy platform, that is, if we've not asked and answered Roger's question.

Besides, when we take this product off the shelf, drawn to it at first by the bedazzling glitter and promise of results, and look at it closely, we don't like what we see. There's just this sense that the core message of the Christian faith sure takes a lot of human effort to get across or, worse, that the core message is lost altogether. Do we really need to entertain people to get them to listen to the gospel? It's been an effective method for drawing in numbers of people, but has it really produced a robust evangelism or robust faith? Play jazz if you want, but play to glorify God in and of itself, not to do evangelism.

Recently I was leading a seminar on evangelism. Since I believe that evangelism is a matter of knowing the gospel and living the gospel, both of which include, when appropriate, speaking the gospel, that's what we talked about. At the end of the seminar a man came up to me and said, "Mack, I'm so grateful for our time. I confess I almost didn't come—usually these seminars make me feel like I'm in training to become an insurance salesman."

Now, I don't have anything against insurance salesmen—or any salesmen for that matter, but I knew what he meant. Somehow there's this feeling that as evangelists we must learn how to

- pitch the message with a careful appeal to self-interest

- promote a program with pizzazz

- overcome hesitancies with a winsome manner

- avoid any offense or problems

- answer objections with humor

- instill fears of losing out

- manipulate conversation to a point of decision

- sign on the dotted line with a sinner's prayer and

- hone our skills to close the deal

Which is fine for insurance, I guess, but Jesus?

For one, Jesus is far too precious to be trivialized that way—and I know Christian insurance agents who agree. So why is it that we keep trying to package the gospel and market it?

Well, because it works, at least if you believe statistics. George Barna reports that 45 percent of Americans in 2006 claim to be born again. That's 130 million people! Yet something seems terribly wrong, since Barna also notes that only 9 percent seem to take what Jesus says seriously in their lives. Many claim Jesus as Lord, but if they don't do what he says, it indicates—according to Jesus—that they aren't his followers in the first place (Luke 6:46).

Could it be that people have prayed a prayer of commitment to the wrong God or agreed to follow something other than Jesus? Maybe they've been led to think that they can take Jesus and mix it with their own way of thinking?

Could it be that people have been persuaded to purchase a bill of goods that doesn't tell the whole story about Jesus in the first place? Maybe much the same as when people purchase, say, an insurance policy without really knowing what it says?

You bet. It happens all the time, with insurance and with Jesus.

So because people are so concerned about results and numbers, their converts often pray to a different God, follow another Jesus, mix Jesus with human thinking without knowing the whole story.

But is that who we want to be as bearers of the good news? Do we want to peddle the gospel (2 Corinthians 2:17)?

No, as evangelists we want to be people who are more concerned with our faithfulness in presenting Christ clearly than we are with results. We want to be the kind of evangelists who take people more seriously than to manipulate them into a prayer of commitment. And we want to be people who present the gospel with care, knowing spiritual lives are at stake.

Okay, so becoming a healthy evangelist is not about what we do, but who we are. We see how pragmatic evangelism can be dangerous to genuine faith. But if it's not pragmatic evangelism what is it? How do we become healthy evangelists?

The first step is to make sure we understand the gospel of Jesus, something a bit more controversial than you might think—the subject of the next chapter.

2

STUDENTS OF THE MESSAGE

Don't Add or Subtract from the Gospel

My friend Clay graduated with honors from a prestigious college in Kentucky. Since he majored in religion, attending seminary was the natural next step. After graduating from the seminary, he took a position as a senior pastor with a small but respectable church in a medium-sized city in the southern United States: First Presbyterian Church. "First Prez" had a growing youth group, and though Clay was busy with the normal work given to senior pastors, he pitched in with the youth. That included helping with a youth retreat at—where else—Disney World.

Clay said one evening he dropped in to a session to hear the speaker who was explaining the gospel to the kids and there had an astounding realization: he had never put his faith in Christ.

Clay had been educated in religion. He had been a good student; he was a nice guy, moral and upright, hard working. His whole life involved religious work. Clay was an ordained pastor in a large denomination. But he was not a Christian, not until there, in an Orlando auditorium, with hundreds of kids, Clay silently, for the first time, repented of his sin and placed his faith in Jesus.

HUMANLY THINKING

How is it that Clay could have missed the gospel? There are many answers, but both Clay and I believe it's because so many have added human thinking to the gospel message.

Such thinking was around even in Jesus' day. When Jesus first reveals to the disciples that he will go to the cross, Peter felt Jesus needed his help to think more clearly. So Peter rebukes Jesus, "Never, Lord! . . . This shall never happen to you." And how did Jesus respond? "You do not have in mind the things of God, but the things of men" (Matthew 16:22-23).

Humanly, Peter couldn't bear to think that Jesus would choose the humiliating way of the cross. The cross was an unnaturally cruel death. It was designed to degrade. It was ugly. It was offensive. But it was the way God chose to redeem the world. Peter wanted to subtract from the plan of God.

We too want to subtract the offense of the cross. We want to guild our crosses and make them more attractive. So we tend to avoid and subtract the messy parts of the gospel about crucifixion, sin and repentance.

Additions to the gospel are as dangerous as subtractions. Be moral, do good deeds, get educated, become religious, belong to a certain denomination. This is human thinking, and it is why Clay's story is repeated around the globe. We must never add to God's declaration that we are Christians by faith, not by works (Ephesians 2:8).

To understand what's at stake for healthy evangelism we must know how to avoid adding or subtracting human thinking to the message of the gospel. To do this we need to know the gospel message through and through. That way we can more easily spot additions or subtractions. Here is an important foundational understanding about the gospel message. It's the encapsulated summary of God's work and our response which leads to salvation. Other things may be important reflections and implications of this message of salvation, but those things are not the gospel message.

THE BAD NEWS

"The gospel," in modern language, means, "Breaking News!" And the news is good news, because there was bad news before. After all, what power is there in "good news" if there was nothing wrong in the first place? And there's plenty of bad news.

Have you heard people say that Christianity is a crutch? They're far too optimistic. We don't need crutches; we need spiritual defibrillators. The fact is, we were born rotten sinners to the core. We may be upright physically, but spiritually, we're dead on arrival. Left to ourselves we have no hope (Romans 5:19; Ephesians 2:1, 12).

It's not that we can't do loving or even amazing things—after all, long ago we were made in the image of God. But these are fleeting and inconsistent moments, and no part of anything we do remains untainted by sin (Luke 18:19; Romans 7:18). We think acts of worldly goodness can mask sin, but they only add to our debt since worldly good deeds fill us with superficial self-righteous pride (Isaiah 64:6), as if we could smile our way out of treason. Our own meager good works could never help us avoid the death sentence that has been pronounced on us. We are chained to sin; we can't help but sin, for it is in our nature (Romans 7:5). And this sin cuts us off from God. In our natural state we rebel against God and all his ways (Isaiah 59:2; Ephesians 4:18)—and this wickedness spits in the face of God (Isaiah 50:6; Mark 14:65). We are as attractive to God as a corpse at a dinner party (Matthew 23:27).

Tough sell, huh?

That's one hard package to market. After all, it's not exactly the generous orthodoxy that speaks to the postmodern world today. Not exactly a message that's going to win friends and influence people, you say. Since this message is difficult to swallow, you can see why pragmatic evangelists leave it out and focus on other parts of the message.

But wait, there's more . . .

As we shake our fist (Job 15:25) at this Creator God, this perfect Holy God, and scheme against his rule, we inflame his wrath and judgment. It's God alone who deals with our lives as he sees fit (Isaiah 45:9; Romans 9:21; Revelation 2:27). But when things go wrong, we get it exactly backwards: we accuse God of evil and act as if it's our right to treat people as a choice—a choice to snub and exploit, and murder. As we speak against God, we breathe out the fumes of rotting flesh, and death hangs about our necks (Romans 3:13).

These pitiful, self-justifying accusations against the Creator

God add to our affront to God—as if we could put God on trial. Every time we accuse God, we reenact the kangaroo court before Pontius Pilate . . . with the same results: the murder of an innocent (John 19:6, 11). We are treasonous rebels who, without constraints, would murder and destroy God himself to establish *ourselves* as God in his place (John 19:15). The astounding story of that trial before Pontius Pilate and subsequent crucifixion is that we are the ones on trial, not Jesus. It's a story of all of us. Don't miss that at the cross we see ourselves in all our sin and evil and wickedness (Isaiah 53:5-6; Romans 3:12, 19). All of us: from Mother Teresa to the lowest, vilest child molester. What awaits us—what we've all earned—is hell.

Does that offend you? Are you angry at these comments? Do you say, "It's not true. I've never been in rebellion with God! It can't be that bad. I'm a good person. What about Gandhi? I love God; we're friends; I'm spiritual; 'my God' would never say such things."

But I contend that if this news, this bad news, offends rather than humbles, you are the one most in danger. For it's not said to offend but to instruct and to warn about a reality—the same warning my doctor might bring of a grave illness, but with far, far greater consequences.

Neither are these merely my opinions. Every thought in these paragraphs comes from the Bible, and these are but samples from an avalanche of indictments about our condition from the Scriptures.

I am well aware of the umbrage people take at such news, Christians included. But why? Doesn't our offense only point to our self-centeredness and self-righteousness? Those very sins we most hate in others?

Actually, our offense convinces me of its truth. The older I get, the less I feel compelled to avoid the subject by hemming, hawing and tiptoeing around, and the more I want people to open their eyes.

To paraphrase G. K. Chesterton, I can't see why people have such problems with original sin; it's the one doctrine for which we have empirical data. Just look at the last 3,500 years of human history.

So what's at stake for healthy evangelism if we subtract from the message of the gospel because people might be offended?

Well, if what you have just read is an accurate picture of our condition, would it not be the cruelest thing to keep it quiet? Would it not lead people to believe that things are much better than they think and one day, at life's end, to approach their Maker and Judge with a false sense of confidence, even bravado?

Furthermore, what right do we have to tailor the message to fit people's tastes? Or to dress up the nice parts to make it sound like we don't have to worry about the bad? I live in the Middle East. I understand why we want to contextualize the message, but to fit the message to context is very different than to *change* the message. To change the message of the gospel comes with the most severe warnings from the apostle Paul (Galatians 1:8).

Besides, it makes for weak disciples of Jesus. People who have a weak view of their own sin, for example, will carry a weak view of grace and love. When Jesus was at the home of Simon the Pharisee, watching the sinful woman wiping his feet with her tears, he said the one who has been forgiven much loves much. And those who have been forgiven little, love little (Luke 7:47). If we don't realize the magnitude of what we've been forgiven, we may identify more with the Pharisee than the woman.

But most importantly, if we do not help people see how dire their condition is, we begin to subtract the need for turning from sin and unbelief. Why do we need to repent when we're not that bad anyway? Yet to subtract repentance is to remove one of the most clearly articulated parts of the gospel from the mouth of Jesus and his apostles (Matthew 3:2; 21:32; Acts 3:19; Romans 2:4; Revelation 3:3).

There's a danger here. We must speak about sin to be true to the message of the good news; after all, there is no good news if there was no bad news first. Yet how do we maintain the balance of explaining sin without seeing evangelism as a process of mere moral reform?

We want people to see their sin in all its horror, not so they are motivated to "clean up their act," but so they fall at the feet of Jesus knowing that he is their only hope. People need to see the depth of their sin so that they come to a fuller understanding of the depth of God's grace.

The sin of the woman who washed Jesus' feet with her tears moved her to humble herself before the religious leaders. Yet it was the one who most looked righteous who was most in need; Simon didn't even believe that Jesus was a prophet, much less God. ("If this man were a prophet, he would have known who and what sort of woman this is who is touching him, for she is a sinner," Luke 7:39 ESV.) He certainly felt no need to fall down at the feet of Jesus. But unrepentant disbelief is the greatest of all sin—that's the sin for which we will be judged.

So we must press home twin truths: our hopeless situation

("apart from me you can do nothing," John 15:5) and amazing grace ("he saved us, not because of righteous things we had done, but because of his mercy," Titus 3:5). I think the sad tendency of well-meaning Christians who want to share their faith is to water down both. They say we're not so bad (you actually *can* clean up your act), and God doesn't really mean it when he says that the unconverted are enemies of God (tut, tut, boys will be boys).

There is a tendency to think that our sins are bigger than our sin—maybe because it's that rare case of language when the plural is smaller than the singular. Sins are those individual acts of rebellion—symptoms of the bigger problem. Our sin is the bigger problem: it's our condition or state which is in hideous rebellion toward a holy and good God. When Christians feel that sins (acts) are bigger than sin (condition), they see evangelism as an effort of moral reform rather than explaining the steps that need to take place to rip out our wicked hearts and replace them with new hearts—that amazing work of God that Jesus called being born again.

God would be perfectly just to let us stumble along in life, trying as best we could to eek out pleasure from the world and then, at death, face his punishment. The fact is we are under God's judgment already (John 3:36). But this God is not a God of justice alone. He is love (1 John 4:8).

God's love is his most magnificent characteristic. This is so assumed in Western culture it's practically lost all meaning, but one thing that distinguishes God's love is how his love, his perfect, tender, self-sacrificing love, holds back his red-hot, scorching wrath.

He does this not by simply sweeping our sin under the rug. There's too much brokenness crying out for his justice for that to happen. Think how many have called to God for justice.

No, he demonstrates his love by sending his Son, Jesus, the Son he loves who is fully God, to live as a man, identify with our human condition, demonstrate through his earthly life as a man what God is like, and then bear the weight of our sin in his own body on the cross (John 3:16).

We see God's holiness satisfied when his love was nailed to the cross. It's the place where God's wrath and love come together—perfectly. Jesus died our death in our place; it was a substitution, a ransom, an act agreed upon by the Father and the Son to pay for the sins of the world, since Jesus was the perfect sacrifice. Jesus became a perfect blood sacrifice for all who would put their faith in him. This is how we gain his forgiveness and his righteousness as well.

Here too is another tempting place to subtract from the message. "How ghastly," some say, "how medieval. What's all this talk about blood and sacrifice and such; aren't we more modern than that?" To accommodate modern sensibilities, many want to explain away the true meaning of the cross, but to do so is to subtract both the depth of God's love and his justice, and do damage to the clear revelation of the Scriptures.

THE GOOD NEWS

After Jesus' death by crucifixion, he was buried in a borrowed grave, and in three days he rose from the dead. His new body bore scars from his crucifixion. The New Testament writers marked his bodily resurrection from the dead as a historical event, and they knew it to be the fulfillment of repeated biblical prophecies over thousands of years.

Today he demonstrates his great love and mercy by reaching into our world, personally, with an offer of life—an offer to individuals to be set free from the bondage of sin and death. It's the offer of life to the dying, those dying under God's judgment, so that the One who would slay us laid down his life to set us free (Romans 5:9).

The Bible is filled with the language of this great offer: prisoners are set free, the lost are found, the blind see, the hungry feast, the dead are given life. This is an offer unique in a world awash with religions, both organized and fabricated. It's not a matter of lineage or rules. In fact, it has nothing to do with any external action you perform. It's a matter of the heart.

So what is this offer of good news?

The offer of the gospel is that our sins—in all their ugliness—can be forgiven and that we can be adopted as God's children with all the earthly privileges and heavenly inheritance of a child of God the Father, by simply turning from sin, especially our sin of unbelief, and placing our complete faith and trust in this Jesus.

That's it?

Yes, that's our response to the offer of God.

To be clear: if we understand this gospel message, and cry out with a wholehearted response of faith to God that we will turn from sin and follow this Christ with perseverance, then we are a Christian. If we do not, or have not, we are not a Christian.

There is vast confusion over what it means to be a Christian, to be a true follower of Jesus in the world today. Many people think they are Christians when they are not because they are following a blend of the gospel and human reasoning. Sadly, on the other hand, I know many people who feel they can't be a Christian because they could never live up to the human requirements.

Human additions to the gospel rob God of his rightful glory. It is easy to feel, like Peter, that God needs our help. And like Peter, we try to add human effort to the gospel. But this allows us to feel that we have had some part in our redemption when it is God alone who has done the work.

Is it any wonder that a constant theme of the New Testament writers was to guard the gospel? Be on your guard that people want to add and to subtract, and therefore know the gospel message so firmly that additions and subtractions become clear. As Paul says, hold firm to the gospel. That's the topic of the next chapter.

3

ON YOUR GUARD

Don't Assume the Gospel

Kevin Roose enrolled at conservative Liberty University as a transfer student from liberal Ivy League Brown University. For one semester at Liberty he presented himself as a believer. He took part in prayer meetings, Bible studies, church choir and even an evangelistic outreach during spring break at Daytona Beach.

But unbeknownst to his fellow students at Liberty, before leaving Brown he had signed a book contract underwriting a secret mission to publish an exposé of conservative evangelicals. Roose entered Liberty as an undercover cultural anthropologist studying a slice of the evangelical world. By his own admission Roose knew very little about Christianity and even less about the evangelical subculture, so he began his semester with fear and trembling.

But when Roose moved into his dorm he discovered, to his amazement, that the students of Liberty were actually real people and then real friends. As the "natives" adopted him as one of their own, Roose began a journey of discovery that is often humorous and highly instructive for any who desire to be healthy evangelists.

It's instructive, for one, to see how easy it was for Roose to fit in. With a couple of tutoring sessions from his one Christian friend back home and a commitment to follow the "Liberty Way," the code of school conduct, Roose quickly passed as a Christian.

After a few weeks Roose says, "At Liberty, see, no one asks me about my faith anymore, so to blend in, I rarely have to do anything more active than keep up my Christian signifiers—going to Bible study, praying before meals, being on time to church. This is what passes for ethical conduct in my world."[1]

Roose blends in so well with the surrounding culture that toward the end of his semester a dorm adviser considers him a "true man of the Lord." Another campus director asks him to be a prayer leader the following year.

Roose said, "I don't know how, but I think I managed to convince most of these guys that I was a strong, faithful evangelical."[2]

The day of reckoning came when the publisher's deadline forced Roose to confess his secret life to his Christian friends:

> In their mental categories of saved and unsaved what I told them took me out of the saved category, but it didn't put me fully in the category of unsaved, either. For a Liberty student, an unsaved person is someone who doesn't get it, who doesn't know how to quote C. S. Lewis or sing "Jesus Paid It All"

without looking at the words. And for them, the fact that I did know these things, that I had gone through the same Christian gauntlet as them, made my story all the more confusing and all the more heartbreaking. My news would have been easier to swallow if I had been a Jew or a Muslim or a steadfast atheist. But to be this close to Christianity for an entire semester and not have accepted Christ? It killed them.[3]

In some ways Roose and his book have become a modern-day parable, and this parable raises interesting questions concerning healthy evangelism. Why was it so easy for Roose to "blend in"? Are superficial "Christian signifiers" all that's needed to pass as a faithful believer today? Why does he come out of Liberty with a view of salvation as a "Christian gauntlet" and not genuine faith?

I think to understand the answers to these questions, we need to understand the process of losing the gospel. Paul wrote Timothy to tell him to guard the gospel. He did that because he was aware that the gospel could be lost. In 2 Timothy 2:2 Paul points to four "generations" of people who are to pass on the gospel: Paul to Timothy, Timothy to faithful people, and faithful people to other faithful people.

These "generations" of Christian leaders might be the next generations of elders in a church. It could apply to the next generations of leaders in a ministry. It might be student generations on a college campus. Regardless, Paul knew if we did not guard the gospel for the next generation, we would lose the gospel.

Recently, while I was speaking with a German Christian about a church building for sale in Berlin, he mentioned they had two potential buyers: a community group and a Muslim fellowship. What happened to the passion that built that church, he wondered. Where did the commitment to the gospel go?

Losing the gospel doesn't happen all at once; it's much more like a four generation process too:

The gospel is accepted →
The gospel is assumed →
The gospel is confused →
The gospel is lost[4]

For any generation to lose the gospel is tragic. But, as Philip Jensen says, the generation that assumes the gospel is the generation that is most responsible for the loss of the gospel. As you can imagine, both an assumed gospel and a confused gospel present particular challenges to healthy evangelism; let's look at ways to deal with both.

ASSUMING THE GOSPEL

When Roose meets Travis, a guy in his dorm, he's surprised to meet an agnostic at Liberty. "I asked him about his lack of faith," said Roose, "I didn't know you weren't a Christian."

Travis smiled. "Most people don't figure it out for a while. If you're a Liberty student, *people just sort of assume you are.*"[5]

They assumed he was a Christian. To assume the gospel is the first step to losing the gospel. An assumed gospel leaves the message of the gospel unspoken and implicit. Assuming the gospel is a lazy forgetfulness that we are in a battle. Don't let the fact that you attend a good church or are involved with a good Christian organization lull you into thinking you don't have to worry about the gospel. The battle against assuming the gospel is ongoing and lifelong.

One of the best reasons never to assume the gospel is that many pretend to possess faith. They may not be doing cultural research, like Roose, but they pretend just the same. They need to see and hear the gospel over time.

Not to sound too simple, but the clearest indication of an assumed gospel is that you don't hear it anymore.

Listen! Was the gospel in the sermon Sunday morning? Could the uninitiated hear that sermon and come to a real faith in Christ? Are gospel principles governing organizational decisions? Do you hear the gospel in people's prayers? Does your fellowship encourage you to say the gospel? And then is it more than just a memorized sketch? Sure, it may follow the form of "God, Man, Christ, Response," but is it in people's own words? Furthermore, do you see it in their actions? Is the gospel lived out? Is membership based on a true commitment to the gospel or just because someone wants to join an organization—or maybe write an exposé?

The healthy evangelist is asking these questions and looking for answers so as to guard the gospel. Here is the critical test. Could you have preached that sermon if Christ had not died on the cross? Could you have developed that Christian leadership principle had Christ not been crucified? I'm not saying be impractical—the Bible has much to say about being practical—but make sure that the practical is tied to the message of Jesus. Otherwise we are on the road to an assumption that will lose the gospel.

Repeating the gospel does wonderful things for us. It challenges those who might be living a double life . . . like Roose. Repeating the gospel affirms the salvation of those who are believers. And it helps us live out the gospel (more about that in chapter four). So don't get tired of repeating the gospel. Don't ever feel like we outgrow the gospel.

People asked Roose about his faith at Liberty, but nobody asked him about his "take" of the gospel message. There was no encouragement to work it out and apply it to life. Consequently, one of the saddest parts of Roose's experience at Liberty was how little he came in contact with the living Christ. Discussions of sex, creation science, marriage, taming the tongue and even evangelism formed the bulk of Roose's experience. Jesus, on the other hand, played a bit part.

Second, when the gospel is assumed, we will place leaders in our churches and organizations based on organizational talent, people skills or academic prowess, but not based on a commitment to the gospel. Do not think asking Roose, an unbeliever, to take part in Christian leadership is an uncommon story. The consequences are horrific, for the result is to mix wolves with sheep (Acts 20:29). When the gospel is no longer the measuring stick for fellowship or Christian leadership, we assume ourselves into confusion.

CONFUSING THE GOSPEL

An assumed gospel opens the door for theological error that quickly leads to a confused gospel. Two errors stand out in Roose's story: moralism and cultural adoption. Let's look at how moralism confuses the gospel.

For Roose to fit into the Christian community only required keeping up his "Christian signifiers." Signifiers included attending a Bible study, praying before meals and being on time to church. The take-home point for Roose? The mark of the Christian was superficial moral behavior. This moralism may be the biggest single counterfeit to true Christian faith.

Don't confuse morality with genuine faith in Christ. Anyone can screw up their discipline and live a seemingly moral life for a time—especially if the issues of the heart are left alone. I know many Muslim friends whose outward morality would shame most Christians. I often hear Christians admire that about Muslims. These Christians act as if praying five times a day could save us. But I think Paul would say, "Who has bewitched you?" just as he did in Galatians 3:1. These Christians mistake the true nature of both the depth of our sin and the greatness of God's grace. Paul says in Colossians that though these things have the appearance of faith, they are counterfeits.

We can confuse all kinds of moral behavior with salvation. This goes right or left. We can confuse pious morality (praying before meals) or moral social action (opposing human trafficking). For that matter we can be moralistic about moralizers. Just as the Pharisee prayed, "God, I thank you that I am not like other men— robbers, evildoers, adulterers—or even like this tax collector" (Luke 18:11), we pray, with no sense of irony, "Oh, God, I thank you that I am not like that judgmental Pharisee."

Make no mistake, good deeds do attest to genuine faith, but they are not faith itself. When it comes to issues of salvation, it's not an overstatement to say that good deeds (from personal piety to social action) without going through the door of the gospel are bad deeds (Romans 14:23). Good deeds without the gospel can fool us, in our pride, to think that our condition is acceptable to God. If people think that their own goodness gets them to God, they are rejecting the core message of the gospel of grace.

The challenge for healthy evangelism is to stop trying to clean people up through rules rather than bring them to the cross.

My friend Pete Hise put himself though seminary by working as a waiter at Applebee's. Each evening when the restaurant closed, the waiters would gather at the bar and have a beer and chat before they went home. Pete saw this as his opportunity. He asked the guys if they would have a Bible study with him if he brought the Bibles. They agreed. Now Pete had signed a statement at his seminary that he would abstain from alcohol, but there was nothing in the contract saying he couldn't be with others who did drink, so Pete began a "Beer and Bible" study. Over the next several weeks, as the power of the Word worked in hearts, waiters began to come to Christ. Lots of them. It was an Applebee's revival.

I appreciate that Pete knew not to start by trying to clean those guys up. He didn't make non-Christians act like Christians. Sure, Pete had to put up with much that offended him—coarse language, racist and sexist jokes, guys who had a couple of beers too many. But Pete understood he was under the law of Christ (1 Corinthians 9:21). Pete did not jettison holy living but, by knowing the difference between moralism and the gospel, Pete saw to it that there are no obstacles to hearing the gospel.

CULTURAL CHRISTIANITY

There was another way the gospel was confused at Liberty. Roose left Liberty feeling that to be a committed believer was to join a culture.

Roose speaks of being saved or unsaved as a "Christian gauntlet" and believes that salvation has to do with the memorization of a hymn and quoting Christian writers rather than a spiritual rebirth. Unfortunately, Roose heard few distinctions between a culture and the gospel. It is easy to do. The gospel can become synonymous with its surrounding culture if we're unclear about the gospel. This can go left and right too. It doesn't matter if it's Republicanism in Lynchburg, or Marxism in Latin America.

I have some rules of thumb that come from living in and writing about various cultures over the years.[6] This is equally applied to things as big as a national culture or as small as a Christian university culture.

- First, remember the Bible critiques culture, not the other way around. That can be difficult, especially when our culture causes blindness. But as a general principle we must be so thoroughly biblical, so steeped in the Scripture, that we can smell out cultural conditions attaching themselves to the gospel. Distinguish between the gospel of Jesus and your particular surrounding culture.[7]

- Be humble about the way your particular culture may have blended with the message of the gospel, causing you to hold worldviews that Jesus would have never required. Remember, culture mimics human nature—that is, we all have the divine image stamped on us, yet all are fallen. There is the godly and the sinful in all cultures. Nothing is sacred about culture.[8]

- Be willing to counter culture; that is, be willing to look different than the culture around you. This is different for different contexts, but keep in mind that Jesus looked countercultural because his culture was "not of this world" (John 8:23-24). We should strive to be resident aliens on earth: living in the world with our citizenship firmly fixed in heaven (Philippians 3:20).

- Never forget the intense pressure to fit into culture. Roose desired to fit in because he had a book contract. For most of us, however, we want to fit in and try to do it by adopting certain cultural norms. Many times cultural norms are morally neutral, but when they begin to obscure or overshadow the gospel, watch out.

The dangerous pattern for healthy evangelism in all of this is that first, an assumed gospel forgets to speak the gospel, and second, a cultural gospel preaches moralism and cultural norms and so twists the gospel's message. Then the gospel is lost altogether.

A Look at How the Gospel Is Lost

What does losing the gospel look like? It starts innocently enough, usually with the assumption that everyone believes and understands the gospel. The result is that members of a church or Christian organization may talk about pressing issues concerning the Christian life, but they don't press into the core message of the Christian faith, the gospel.

Since no one is talking about the gospel and since it is no longer the measure of the ministry, the uncommitted (or even nonbelievers) who are moral and organized people (just like Roose) fill leadership positions.

If it can happen at Liberty, it can happen anywhere—in a church or a sports outreach program, in a mission agency or in serving the poor. Soon the gospel is trivialized; after all, the good news is something you learned way back in Sunday school—you know, something for the kids. And the goal is to be good, moral people isn't it? Of course, that depends on the moral concern of the day—pick one: global warming or praying before meals.

This quickly becomes the culture around you, and in a few short generations, the gospel is lost and the organizations are simply shells that once held the gospel. Sports outreach programs can go the way of the YMCA. Missionary agencies can go the way of the Student Volunteer Movement.[9] Gospel ministry to the poor goes the way of the Salvation Army. Churches become museums or mosques, and Christian colleges become . . . Brown University.

It's the height of irony that Roose attended Brown, a university founded a couple of hundred years ago by Christians who would not look that different in their theology than a Jerry Falwell today. At Brown's inception, twenty-two of the thirty-six Brown University trustees were required to be Baptists; the rest were other denominations. But somewhere in their history, the gospel was assumed, then confused, and eventually lost. So much so that Roose could say, "I was a student at Brown University, a school known for everything Liberty is not. In fact, it wouldn't be unfair to call the schools polar opposites."[10]

Make certain you don't lose the gospel. Guard it carefully by never assuming and never confusing the gospel.

47

4

DOES THE MESSAGE WE SHARE LOOK LIKE THE MESSAGE WE BEAR?

Living the Implications of the Gospel

Three men sat in my living room with me. Across from me sat my pastor, John. On my right and left sat two high-powered businessmen. Skilled and toughened over the years from international business, these two gave cold and hard glances at each other. Briefcases filled with legal poison bulged at both their feet. On my right sat the successful owner of the business; on my left, the aggrieved employee. Lawsuits had been filed. And they were members of our church.

"Gentlemen," I said, turning to the man on my left, "I want to start by saying that we are gathered here to ask you, Mike, to drop your lawsuit against Robert. You understand 1 Corinthians 6: You are not allowed to take this case to a Muslim court."

Mike looked down and fingered his legal papers, written in Arabic script.

Turning to the man on my right, "And Robert, though you are under no compulsion to do so, after Mike drops the case, we would like you to be generous beyond the obvious amounts this case would cost you."

Robert's face flushed: "He has no case at all. The three hundred thousand he requires is absurd . . ."

Mike growled, "I believe my lawyers will help you find out just how good my case . . ."

"Wait," I interrupted, sensing I was losing control. "Before we go any further I want to say that it's not the legal or financial issues that are of first concern here. It's that we are coming together to sit at the foot of the cross and work this out."

That's how we start living out the implications of gospel—at the cross.

THE A TO Z OF CHRISTIANITY

So far we've seen that healthy evangelists understand the dangers of pragmatic evangelism. Healthy evangelists avoid tailoring the gospel to fit human sensibilities and human reason. We get a stranglehold on the message of the gospel and are then able to recognize any addition or subtraction from the gospel. We also guard the gospel by making sure we never assume the gospel message.

The next mark of the messenger is understanding how to live out the gospel in all of life. What does that look like? That's what my two high-powered business friends, my pastor and I were trying to work out.

Many feel the gospel is what gets you saved. Then we focus on other things in the Christian life, such as raising our kids, working on Christian marriage and going on short-term mission trips.[1]

But as Tim Keller says, "We never get beyond the gospel in our Christian life to something more advanced. The gospel is not the first step in a stairway of truths; rather, it is more like the hub in a wheel of truth. The gospel is not just the A-B-C's but the A to Z of Christianity. The gospel is not just the minimum required doctrine necessary to enter the kingdom, but the way we make all progress in the kingdom."[2]

Problems arise for Christians because we do not connect the deep implications of the gospel in all parts of our life. Practicing these principles helps us to watch our doctrine closely, as Paul instructs Timothy and us (1 Timothy 4:16).

In the same verse, Paul instructs us to watch our lives too; we must make sure that we understand what it means to live a gospel-centered life, to live out the implications of the gospel in the day to day.

It is the height of irony that our approach to the world in witness would look different from the gospel. It's the gospel we're sharing—how could our presentation of the message be inconsistent with the message? Yet often the message is shoehorned into a canned presentation that is completely opposite of what we say we believe, or often the grace we offer in witness looks different than the life we live.

Many Christians rebel against the obvious hypocrisy of "inconsistent evangelism," and so they tend to keep quiet, not wanting to be associated with the prejudices and stereotypes which arise from bad witnesses, but that's inconsistent too.

Jesus came preaching. And the life of Jesus was completely consistent with the message he brought: he was bold; he did not fear what people thought of him; he did not even worry about the consequences of the truth he shared. He trusted in the Father's care.

The apostle Paul was consistent. Paul desired "that whenever I open my mouth, words may be given me so that I will fearlessly make known the mystery of the gospel" (Ephesians 6:19). When he said hard things he was able to remind those who knew him how consistent his life was with the gospel (Acts 20:18; 2 Timothy 3:10).

So make sure the message you share is consistent with the message you bear. Endeavor, by God's grace, to think through how to keep careful watch over your life as well as your doctrine by living out the gospel.

In one sense, anyone who knows the gospel knows this in his or her heart. When I said to Mike and Robert, "We're going to sit at the foot of the cross," everyone in the room felt the weight of the gospel. Contained in this one sentence was a plea to put the brutal requirements of law aside. It was about treating others with grace, just as we received grace from God. It was about forgiveness, undeserved. It was about reconciliation . . . it was the gospel lived out.

We looked at the gospel message in the last chapter, and it roughly follows the outline of our condition, God's character, Christ's work of salvation and our response. These are the basic components of the gospel message. You can say it in a minute; it takes a lifetime to live. Here's an important distinction. The gospel message is the crystallized key components of the gospel—compressed as one might compress carbon into a diamond. In this way the gospel message is protected, and the message of salvation by faith alone is clear to those who would come to Christ.[3] But the gospel is not just a way of salvation. There are fantastic and wonderful implications of the gospel that explode into meaning when we live out the gospel. It's the diamond unpacked in our lives. The implications of the gospel are critical to becoming who we are meant to be as healthy evangelists. This is the way to have evangelism integrated into our lives, rather than as an add-on accessory.

As Richard Lovelace says, "Most people's problems are just a failure to be oriented to the gospel—a failure to grasp and believe it through and through."[4]

Paul asks the Galatians: "After beginning with the Spirit, are you now trying to attain your goal by human effort?" (Galatians 3:3). We answer, with Paul, "No!" We don't start with a work of grace in our lives and then leave grace to grow by our own human effort. We need to grow spiritually by pressing into the gospel of grace, not moving away from it. Yet how often we teach that while we're justified by grace, we grow by works and human effort.

That was certainly the message I was taught. As a new Christian I thought I was saved by grace, but to grow I needed to work out my salvation.[5] "Thanks, God," I'd say with a spiritual salute. "I'll take it from here."

Is it any wonder, then, that after a number of years of trying to grow in my own power, it took crawling back to the cross to once again remember his grace? Remember, first and foremost, all of God's work in our lives is a work of grace.

We must always be on our guard against the natural, but dangerous, tendency to revert to the law rather than live by the gospel of grace. To be sure, there are commands or imperatives we are to follow and practice as believers.[6] But to practice inner spiritual disciplines or outer social consciousness in our own power is a quick road to exhaustion and sin. To miss the link between the gospel of grace and our growth in Christ moves Christians into either self-righteousness or rank hedonism.

We are saved by faith and we grow by faith. As Michael Lawrence says, "We can not separate the imperatives of the gospel from the grace of God at the cross of Christ."

GOING DEEPER INTO THE GOSPEL

So how do we establish a link between the message of the cross and living life? We must push deeper into the meaning of the cross to bring us closer to the heart of God. Just as the cross of Christ is at the center of the gospel, so living out a cross-centered life is the center of spiritual growth.[7]

Go deeper into the gospel. Don't grow away from it—ever. The real work in our spiritual growth is to allow the themes of the gospel to permeate our lives. We cycle though periods of deep looks at our sin, taking those sins and nailing them to the cross, receiving deep love, grace and mercy in Christ, and starting again. We never grow beyond the gospel.

The following are examples of how we might link our lives with the message of the cross:

54

- Seeing the depth of our forgiveness by God at the foot of the cross allows us to forgive others and guards us from self-condemnation too.

- Knowing that we have been reconciled to God by the cross calls us to be people of reconciliation.

- Knowing that God did not spare even his own Son on the cross tells us we are deeply loved and that we can rely on God's will for our lives without fear.

- Being accepted by God though the cross allows us to be obedient out of joyful gratitude, not out of duty.

- Knowing that we have been adopted as sons and daughters as a result of the work on the cross guards us from living as independent orphans alone in the world.[8]

In the book of Galatians, Paul tells a story of how he rebuked the apostle Peter, because Peter was forgetting the gospel (Galatians 2). Peter? Forgetting the gospel? If anyone was to understand the gospel it would be Peter, who spent years with Jesus personally, saw his miracles, his death and resurrection, and had experienced Christ's forgiveness for his own sin of denying Christ in his hour of greatest need. Yet Paul says that Peter was "not acting in line with the truth of the gospel" (Galatians 2:14).

What specifically merited a rebuke? Perhaps Peter feared how his own people, the Jews, might respond to him, a "fear of man" problem. Perhaps there were residual hints of racism as he began to favor the Jewish Christians over the Gentile Christians. D. A. Carson points out that Peter might have even had it in mind that his actions would cause persecution back in Jerusalem.[9] But clearly in Paul's mind, Peter was hypocritically siding with those who wanted to add Jewish law to the gospel. So Paul sharply rebuked Peter, and we should rejoice because Paul says that as a result the truth of the gospel was preserved for us (Galatians 2:5).

But notice Paul's principle for the rebuke: "not acting in line with *the truth of the gospel*." Don't miss this. Paul, in this verse, sets out the rule of life. Our lives need to be lined up with, in accord with, the gospel. As we've seen before, the gospel is not only about salvation. The gospel is how we live every day.

So how is it that fear, racism or law were not the gospel? Fear takes the place of belief. Racism is worldly systematic oppression of people based on prejudice. The law condemns, but has no power to save. All at odds with the principles of the gospel: faith, freedom and love.

If Peter missed the gospel as a way of life, how much more can we? If Peter forgot the gospel, how much more can we?

How little has changed? We still have a fear of what others think of us, and we still find it easy to side with those who would add law to the gospel to earn our way into God's favor. We are still prone to think that we need law to make us grow.

So we must repeat the message of grace to one another because we too often forget.

And to put this in practice actually does have much to do with all points of life, even raising our kids, or our marriages. C. J. Mahaney tells the story of rebuking his teenage son for some family infraction. But later his wife, Carolyn, commented to him that though he was right in his assessment of the situation, "I didn't hear the gospel in your rebuke." She rightly understood how to link the gospel with living out the implications of the gospel.

I was with a pastor in his study while he was talking on the phone. I only heard one side of the story, but he was speaking with a man whose wife had had an affair. The pastor was pleading with the man to live a life according to the gospel. "Forgive her," he said, "sin is the expectation. Grace is the unusual thing in the world. If she is truly repentant, then forgive her." He hung up the phone and looked at me and said, "I don't think he understands the gospel." The pastor wasn't sure that the husband knew how to live out the gospel—not the woman who had committed the grievous offense, but the man who had an unforgiving heart.

Of course, acting in line with the gospel has enormous implications for healthy evangelism. For the healthy evangelist, living out the gospel forms our approach to the world in witness.

- The gospel shapes our view of people, since we know (to paraphrase C. S. Lewis) that being a son or daughter of Adam is enough to bow the head of any king and lift the head of any beggar.

- We do not ask, "What is ethical?" or "What is moral?" but instead ask ourselves, "Is this in line with the message of the gospel?"

- We share our faith with joy, since our hearts are filled with gratitude about Christ's work in us.

- We can be generous with our faith since we know God's generous love.

- We do not fear the rejections of others since we know our acceptance is by God.

- We witness with humility since salvation is by grace alone.

- We share without manipulation because true faith is from God alone and cannot be manipulated.

- We share freely with all because we know he redeemed *us;* as a result, there can't be difficult cases beyond the grace of God.

- Our proclamation of the gospel is filled with truth and grace because our message is filled with grace and truth.

When our lives are in line with the gospel and our witness to Christ is consistent, we find that our grace-filled lives have perfume-like attraction (2 Corinthians 2:16). Don't be surprised at the opportunities God will bring your way to share your faith. And as you share your faith, you become the instrument that God uses to move people from death to life.

Back in my living room with the two businessmen and my pastor, Mike said, "Well, if I cancel the legal proceedings what guarantee do I have that Robert will pay?"

"None," I said. "But we are not trusting in Robert. We are trusting in Christ."

"Okay," he said, softly. "I'll do that. I can trust him."

Touched with Mike's willingness to lay aside the lawsuit, Robert leaned forward. "My board has only authorized for me to pay fifty thousand, but Mike, I am willing to pay out of my own pocket over the next number of months another two hundred."

"And Mike, if you are willing to trust in Christ by following the principle of 1 Corinthians 6, then the church is willing to help from our benevolence fund," said Pastor John.

Mike's chin fell to his chest and he said, "Would you really do that for me?" he said. He began to weep.

When we sit at the foot of the cross and live it out, we will see the power of the gospel. Maybe not as dramatically as two tough business guys blubbering in my living room—but in the hearts of others before the throne of heaven, it's even more dramatic than that. To sit at the foot of the cross is to witness the power of the gospel unfolding in our lives.

5

MESSENGERS IN A TROUBLED WORLD

The Gospel and Social Change

"This is where they killed my grandfather," Kim translated.

Kim, a freshman from Colorado State University, stopped dead on the narrow rocky path on the ridge of the hill, her eyes growing wide. She brushed back her brown hair swirling around her face in the high, warm winds. She asked for clarification from the Ixil girl, a Mayan descendant who was about Kim's age.

As they talked, I glanced at the shallow cave in the side of the hill, suspecting what it represented. Hawks circled overhead; smoke from the slash-and-burn farming whipped over the ridge and mixed with the blue haze covering the brown and green quilt-like farms on the horizon.

"Yes," Kim said, turning to me with hand outstretched toward the cave, her other hand on top of her head to hold down her hair;

her eyes remained transfixed on the girl. "That cave is where they murdered her grandfather and twenty other men from the church." Kim's voice quivered. The last word in her sentence squeaked out with a bit of question mark: "men from the . . . church?"

The Ixil girl laughed, oddly, at Kim's shock, but her eyes brimmed with tears. Then her story poured out.

Kim tried to keep up with the torrent of Spanish. "She's talking too fast, but I think they came in helicopters and surrounded a prayer meeting . . . shoot to kill orders . . . dangerous. She says they saved bullets and used knives, something about stuffing them in that cave . . . oh," she choked out, "this is horrible." And she broke down unable to talk. The young Ixil girl put her arm around Kim to comfort her . . . to comfort Kim!

I watched the hawks high above.

As the realization of where we stood gripped the group, another student sobbed. Some began to pray silently. But mostly it became quiet, very quiet, except for the wind. We stood at the site of yet another mass grave in the Ixil area of Guatemala.

The war there had been partly theological experiment, largely tribal and fully genocidal.

"This is holy ground," I said quietly. "Let's pray for awhile."

Someone had the presence of mind to snap a picture while we prayed. I have it framed on my desk. Our heads are bowed. My son, about thirteen at the time, is praying next to me. Some students are prostrate. We're on the rocky outcrop of a high point of a hill. When I look at the picture, it's as if I can smell the smoky air of that faraway day, and relive the shock of those twenty or so students, most of whom were struggling for the first time with rank injustice.

I've spent much of my life trying to reach people in tough places. How many mass graves have I walked by in the Ixil area? Still, the rush of memories from that picture makes me feel the day with such intensity that it could have been yesterday, and it makes me cry. I didn't cry then, but I do now.

As those students stood on that mountaintop, they began to piece together the connections of injustice: the horrific thought, for example, that every cute orphan we cuddled in the orphanage represented two ugly murders. These connections invariably raise questions. They bubble up in various forms, asked innumerable ways.

The first question usually takes the form: "What can I do?" In the face of such hurt and pain, we must be very careful with our answers, but there is never a more important time to understand who we are to be.

Other questions bubble to the surface, usually subsets of the first: "How can I share the gospel with people who have faced such injustice and know such suffering?" After all, isn't it true that "a hungry man has no ears"?[1] "Isn't it 'the gospel' to just take care of their needs?"

EVANGELISM FOR THE BRUTALIZED

For years Christians have separated social action and the gospel message. Yet to separate the gospel message and social action is to assume that the gospel doesn't produce social change. But the gospel brings social change *in and of itself.* Actually, it could be argued that the gospel has brought the greatest social change the world has ever known. So avoid falsely separating social action from evangelism; evangelism produces a true act of social action. To know this helps us answer the first question, "What can I do?" The answer is to carefully tell people who have been treated brutally, or who live in deprivation, the good news of Christ.

When our missionary friend Mike McComb tried to introduce protein into the diets of the largely illiterate Guatemalan farmers, it was a masterful combination of expertise, training and strategy. He started his work toward the end of the murderous civil war. Mike faithfully shared the gospel too. And Mike noticed it was the gospel that allowed for protein to get to the people.

When the gospel was understood and accepted in villages, Mike reported, men stopped getting drunk and beating their wives. As they attended church they started to attend to their crops as well as their children's education. Tomas, the mayor of Nebaj,[2] told me that it was only when the gospel came to the Ixil lands that real change happened.[3] Mike says that the preaching of the gospel did more to eliminate hunger than fish farms or crop rotation ever did. We must never forget that the gospel brings more long-term social good than any governmental program ever developed.

Do the hungry have ears? You bet they do. In my experience those whose ears seem most closed to the gospel are not the hungry but the stuffed and self-indulgent. We have much to say to those who have faced injustice. We must never forget that the best thing that can happen for anyone is to know the living God. The question is not how can we share the gospel with the oppressed and hungry, but how could we *not* share the gospel with the oppressed and the hungry since the gospel brings the greatest message of true hope for an oppressed and hungry world?

Remember that all gospel themes cry out with new meaning in the face of injustice: the terror of sin, the need for reconciliation, a sacrificial loving God on a cross. All these explode with meaning in the midst of the ills of the world.[4] Jesus is far more relevant to refugees in Africa since he fled to Africa as a child with his family. Jesus is far more relevant to those who suffer torture and death unjustly since he suffered torture and death unjustly. To know that Jesus promises perfect justice on the day of his return gives hope beyond understanding to those who have been brutalized—not pie in the sky hope, but hope with sufficient evidence to lay down our lives.

So to be who we are meant to be we must remember any desire to distance speaking the gospel into pain and deprivation is a result of a whole host of misguided impulses, Western guilt for one. We must remember that to be who we are meant to be in Christ is to speak the hope of the gospel into a hurting world.

We need to see the spiritual needs of others. We must confess that pain, deprivation and injustice at times seem to trump the message of the gospel and when this happens we see the naked thinness of our faith, and how we don't believe the gospel through and through. We expose how sold out to materialism we've become when material suffering dashes our faith. Confronted by the death of a malnourished baby or exploitive greed in human trafficking, we forget the reality of the deep triumph over injustice at the cross and its promise of perfect justice on "the Day" when Christ returns and makes all things right. Far from forgetting the brokenness of the world, God intimately joined us in our horrific pain. We forget that for those who suffer, our answers are better than any the world has ever offered.

In Luke 10:29, a lawyer asks a question that sets the stage for Jesus to tell the story of the good Samaritan: "Who is my neighbor?" Put another way, the lawyer wants Jesus to put restrictions on who we are to love. In the parable, Jesus makes it clear that just as the "Samaritan loved the wounded man, we as Christians are called upon to love *all* men as neighbors, loving them as ourselves."⁵ The point: all people are our neighbors—everyone. That's because all people have the mark of the divine in them. Jesus is helping the lawyer, and us, see that when we love others we are moving from how the world sees people to how God sees people.

Our calling as Christians is to love our neighbor. As J. I. Packer says, "The nature of love is to do good and to relieve need. If, then, our neighbor is unconverted, we are to show love . . . by seeking to share with him the good news without which he will perish. So we find Paul warning and teaching 'everyone' (Col 1:28) not merely because he was an apostle, but because every man was his neighbor."⁶ Our call is to share the gospel with everyone, hungry or full.

It's notable that scriptural directions for sharing our faith in the New Testament are often coupled with directions to correct our views of people. So Jesus talks with a wayward Samaritan woman— to her amazement and that of the disciples. At the same time he tells the disciples to open their eyes to the harvest, a harvest they missed because of their racist/sexist view of people (John 4:9, 35). Jesus' last words on earth were a directive to make disciples of all nations, or ethnicities, a command so strange it took direct intervention with Peter later, in a vision, to confirm that God's call is to all people without partiality (Matthew 28:18-20; Acts 10:9-36).

Peter would later tell believers to "always be prepared to give an answer to everyone who asks you to give the reason for the hope that you have," while instructing that we not fear what people fear (1 Peter 3:13-15). Paul knew that Jesus was a light to all nations, as foretold by Isaiah (49:6), but it took hard times from his own people to move him to the Gentiles (Acts 13:46-47). Later he explains how his passion for the salvation of all compelled him to give up his rights so nothing would stand in the way of the gospel, the gospel for people who were different than Paul (1 Corinthians 9:19-23). In the most direct link of evangelism and a Godlike view of people, Paul commanded the Corinthians to stop viewing people from a worldly standpoint when sharing the gospel, reminding them that that same worldly attitude justified crucifying Christ (2 Corinthians 5:16). Though we are to be wise with outsiders, Paul would say, we are to make the most of every opportunity to share our faith (Colossians 4:5-6).

As we trace these passages from the Gospels though Acts and the Epistles, we see directives to share our faith joined with corrective, loving views of those around us. Re-envisioning those around us is of the first order in healthy evangelism.

IS MEETING PHYSICAL NEEDS EQUAL TO THE GOSPEL?

Packer is right to say that the nature of love is to relieve need. This includes physical needs too. So in the same way we are called to relieve spiritual needs, and just as we must see all people as God sees people, we are also compelled to meet physical challenges in the material world.

At different times in history, Christians applied the gospel toward the social ills of their times differently. Reading the Scripture in a common language, ending slavery and creating just laws all required different social actions springing from the same gospel. Our world today comes with situations which require us to respond, be it introducing more protein into diets to stop babies from dying of malnourishment in Guatemala or trying to stop tin-pot dictators from brutalizing believers for their faith in North Africa or putting an end to the sex slave trade in Southeast Asia.

Again, our responses take different forms. Do I take part in seeing these ills end regardless of the evangelistic opportunity it affords? With all my heart, yes and amen. We care for others regardless of any return for our efforts—evangelistically or otherwise. We never qualify whom it is we are to love.

Given these situations, both in yesteryear and today, it is easy to understand why some want to call social action "the gospel" since caring for others so deeply parallels the gospel's message. It's a part of love and it's a function of redemption. And certainly all Christians are called to care for others. But actually the question "Isn't it the gospel to take care of needs?" exposes our difficulty in believing the gospel through and through.

Clarity is critical here. Because the themes of the gospel are so powerful in the face of suffering and injustice in the world, it's tempting to call living out the gospel "the gospel."

So, is caring for others "the gospel"? Is that evangelism? No, not without the spoken message of the gospel of Jesus. The gospel message is the message that produces salvation. So we should never confuse meeting physical needs with sharing the gospel.

Caring for others represents the gospel, it upholds the gospel, it points to the gospel, it's an implication of the gospel, but it is not the gospel, and it is not equal to the gospel.

Furthermore, all actions of kindness, compassion and justice must be done with the hope to share our faith, otherwise we are not upholding the gospel. We share the good news always open to doing good, and we do good always with the hope of sharing our faith. We never divorce the two.

If we get nothing in return, it's okay because it is the nature of love. But do not forget that seeing people come to Christ in the midst of suffering and injustice is to do the greatest good we could ever do. To misunderstand this is to be blinded by cultural, materialistic worldviews rather than to believe in the power of the gospel.

The consequences for elevating social action to an equal status with meeting material needs can be grave. A Swedish friend doing Ph.D. research on the aftermath of liberation theology's war[7] in Guatemala commented, "I am worried that people don't understand the danger of mixing worldly thinking with bits of Christian theology . . . well-intentioned Christians supported a kind of social action which called for a resistance movement. That's why there was murder in the streets in Nebaj." Murder of people such as the grandfather of a young Ixil girl who stood with us on a mountaintop in Guatemala.

To be healthy in our evangelism, when we see those places racked with poverty or unjust political leaders or oppressive regulations toward people of faith, remember we work for those around us out of love and compassion, never requiring a response to the gospel, but with a deep and heartfelt desire that our work of love be redemptive and point to the message of Christ's ultimate work of redemption. And we never hold back from boldly sharing our faith.

6

WAVING THE FLAG

Understanding True Biblical Conversion

Because the UAE is an expressly Muslim nation, only one official evangelical Protestant church exists in Dubai where we live. Being forced into one church results in what so many long to be—multieverything: multinational, multiethnic, multicultural. It's a taste of heaven.[1]

Our church takes membership seriously. This goes against the grain of much modern thinking about church membership, as many churches want to do away with membership altogether. But it's simple, really. The Church consists of followers of Christ (Ephesians 2:19-22), and Christ calls his followers to commit to each other (John 13:34-35). Membership is a visible expression of our love for Christ and his people. Besides, it's biblical. The early church had votes, and how could they have

a vote if they didn't have membership (2 Corinthians 2:6)?
Simple.

Well, sort of.

Part of the process for membership is for people to meet with one of the church leaders or elders and talk about their commitment of faith. Some people have clear commitments to Christ; for others, it's clear they are not Christian.[2] Those two types are easy. But one of the toughest things I do is talk to people who are in the muddled middle.

Who are the converted?

I feel my heart sink to my shoes when it becomes clear to me that good people, well-meaning people, churchgoing people have been convinced that they are Christians but are not. Since our church in Dubai consists of communities of people from sixty nations and from as many church and unchurched backgrounds as you can imagine, I can say confidently, this issue spans the nations, crosses generations and is broadly interdenominational.

What marks conversion? How should we judge (or judge not lest we be judged)?[3] It's not so simple, which is perhaps the real reason many churches are abandoning membership.

Often views of conversion result from our own experience, but does that mean everyone must come to Christ in the same way? Does it require a show of hands? Is conversion a long journey? Do you have to be baptized in a certain church? Must one say a specific prayer, or a prayer at all? More broadly, does our view of conversion stem from culture or what is modeled in one church or merely what we think?

How we answer these questions will shape our practice of evangelism. Our answer, to be healthy evangelists, is to understand true biblical conversion, without which our evangelistic efforts will be misshapen.

Here are five principles of biblical conversion which must be understood.

1. CONVERSION IS REQUIRED

There are many who would think that conversion is simply unnecessary. They even see the word *conversion* as derogatory. Not the New Testament, however. Paul honors the first convert in Asia (Romans 16:5) and reports joyfully of conversions to the church leaders in Jerusalem (Acts 15:3). We should see it the way Paul does because conversion is a requirement to be a Christian. Jesus made it clear to Nicodemus that without conversion you cannot enter into the kingdom of God (John 3:3). No one is born a Christian. "God has no grandchildren," as the saying goes. Jesus said that we *must* be born again. Put another way, Jesus tells us that we need the spiritual equivalent of a heart transplant (Ezekiel 11:19).

So people aren't Christians because they were baptized in a certain church or have a long lineage of Christians in the family or come from a certain part of the world. It is only the work of God in hearts that brings people to repent and believe the work of Christ on the cross.

When we understand that conversion is required for all, we avoid the mistake of assuming people are Christian because they seem to be morally upright, a member of our denomination or from a strong Christian family.

Perhaps you have had the experience of asking people if they were a Christian and they acted offended, as if you had accused them of being someone who lived in the gutter. But a *Christian* is not synonymous with "good person." In fact, for the unconverted, "being good" can be a hindrance to conversion (Luke 18:18-23). There are many good people in churches who are not converted. This is sadly common, so much so that church pews are flooded with people who think they are Christians when they are not.

2. CONVERSION REQUIRES UNDERSTANDING

Many think a deeply moving spiritual experience is conversion. I'm regularly around Hindu people who have powerful spiritual encounters. I've been to Muslim Sufi religious gatherings where the spiritual experiences are mystical and deep. Spiritual experiences are a dime a dozen.

But true converts to Christ *understand* that they are sinners. They *know* they must repent and place their heartfelt faith in Christ's work on the cross. Converts *understand* what Jesus has done on the cross.[4] They may not know the words *justification* or *atonement*, but they *understand* that our sins have been placed on Christ for the payment of sin to purchase us back into a right relationship and right standing with God (1 Corinthians 2:12).

Don't misunderstand me; true conversion is a deeply profound spiritual event—always. We have moved from slavery to freedom, after all. But a spiritual experience without understanding only mimics genuine faith. And unfortunately, as marketers have discovered, it's easier to mimic faith by manipulating emotions and focusing on emotional responses rather than making sure someone understands the message.

Knowing that conversion and understanding are linked provides us with safeguards too. For one, it helps us not confuse mere spiritual interest with conversion. We check and make sure people understand the terms and the concepts of the gospel. We take questions seriously and try to answer them as best we can from the Scripture.

Caring for the mind guards us from treating conversion as if it's a magic formula. Too many think of a raised hand, the sinner's prayer, even baptism as a charm that gets people into heaven. But without proper understanding, the only place those things get us is confusion.

All this means that the healthy evangelist takes care to teach the gospel message in its entirety. That means we should explain, listen, answer objections, lay out facts. In short, we should teach so people can understand. This is why Paul's method in evangelism (which he describes in Colossians 1:28), as J. I. Packer says, was primarily a "teaching method."[5]

3. True Conversion Requires Genuine Faith

As Paul Little said, faith is only as good as the object in which that faith is placed.[6] Understanding is not enough. There must be heartfelt, deep-seated faith and trust in Christ, his work and his call to us personally. This is faith that moves the mountains of our hearts to cry out to God to save us. This is the same sort of faith that one might have when you step on a 747 and believe that a massive hunk of metal will hurtle you though the air safely. It's the same sort of faith that goes through a green light trusting that other drivers will stop for a red light in the intersection. This is the faith that allows doctors to cut us open and rearrange our insides with the hope that we will awake better off. In other words, it's the kind of faith that entrusts our lives to another.

4. A RADICALLY CHANGED LIFE
ATTESTS TO TRUE CONVERSION

Someone recently said to me, "Why, of course, Mack, I believe in the resurrection, but let's not get carried away." Not get carried away? About a dead man coming back to life? If we can't get carried away about that, what can we get carried away about? If there is not some wonder about the glory of God, there should be some wonder about whether a true conversion has happened.[7]

On the deepest level you cannot be truly converted and avoid a radically changed life, for you have moved from death to life. Of course, what is radical for one is trivial for another, but usually the change is marked by a deep desire to obey God and to do his will. It may take different expressions for different people, but it is a radical change nonetheless.[8]

Luke links obedience with faith when he says that priests "became obedient to the *faith*" (Acts 6:7, my emphasis). Paul sees deeds as a litmus test of true conversion when he says to Titus there are many rebellious people who "claim to know God, but by their actions they deny him" (Titus 1:15-16). And James writes that anyone who claims belief but does not show it with deeds has aligned themselves with the demons (James 2:19).

The requirement of a changed life guards us from "easy believism"—giving mere mental assent to the facts of Jesus, but with unmoved hearts and will.

Understanding that a changed life is required to attest to true conversion also guards us from thinking that the only important event is the conversion event. This provides us with a check to our evangelism: if many are responding to Jesus, but few are changed, we can be sure there is something wrong with the message.[9] The ultimate mark of conversion, as I've heard Mark Dever rightly say, is not walking an aisle, but picking up a cross.

5. CONVERSION RESULTS FROM GOD'S ACTION

Many feel conversion depends on the individual's free will. But Jesus states clearly that we didn't choose him. He chose us (John 15:16, see also 2 Thessalonians 2:13). The modern Christian community grossly overstates "free will"—a phrase not found in the Bible.

Think. It is the Holy Spirit who works in our hearts to make us aware of God. It is the Holy Spirit who convicts us of sin. God is the one who gives us the spiritual ability to cry out with saving faith. And, as we've seen in previous chapters, it is Jesus alone who has done the work of justification for us. After death we will stand before God and give him all glory for what he has done—not what we have done. God does the work, including calling us to himself.[10]

People don't come to faith because of the excellence of our presentation or because we provided the perfect circumstance.[11] People come to genuine faith because God draws them. This guards us from thinking that we can manufacture conversions in the following important ways:

- When we understand that it's God's work in people's lives, we avoid the mistake of working hard on performance at the expense of prayer; it leads us to pray and trust in the One who can produce a converted heart. (As Acts 2:47 tells us, it was the *Lord* who added to their numbers daily.)

- Understanding that God is the one who works in conversion guards us from thinking that results are more important than faithfulness to the message. If we, in our own power, could create situations causing people to convert, we would stoop to any tactic or trickery to simply get people "converted." But God is in control, so we trust in the power of the message and the Holy Spirit to do the work in hearts (Romans 1:16). Our job is to be faithful to the message. So we never hide the hard parts of the gospel as we talked about in chapter two. We are not afraid of our own limitations, which we will talk about in the next chapters. And there is no need to appeal to felt needs. Evangelism that appeals to a felt need is often an appeal to the sinful nature, rather than an offer to let God slay sinful nature.

- Knowing we cannot manufacture converts guards us from guilt and workaholism. When we blow it in evangelism, spiritual lives are still in the hands of God. If it was up to our own efforts, we would do nothing else but devote ourselves to full-time evangelism, since a person's salvation rested on us. But since conversion is in the hands of God, we are motivated by the privilege of being used by God to spread the gospel.

- Understanding that God is the one who works in conversion guards our hope. It's easy to think that many are beyond human effort, but no one is beyond God's ability to save. So we never lose hope.

- And knowing it's God's action that brings conversion makes sure we give thanks and glory to the right person—Jesus. The idea that people can choose God apart from his work in their lives is actually an affront to God as it robs God of the glory rightfully due to him (Ephesians 2:8).

"Hey, Dad," our youngest son, seventeen, shouted from his room.

"Yes, Isaac," I said.

"Remember when they taped a white flag to the bottom of our chairs at a church back in the States and I was eight and the speaker told us to wave the flag around if we wanted to surrender to God?"

"Sorta. I remember you waving it around," I said, walking into his room.

He was studying *Christian Beliefs* by Wayne Grudem, highlighter in hand. He was getting ready to meet with the youth pastor.

"You didn't take that very seriously, did you?" he asked.

"Well, we took *you* seriously, but no, not really. I guess we didn't think it was for you; I mean, what eight-year-old doesn't want to wave a flag? But why do you ask?"

"Um, thanks. You were right. I didn't know what I was doing."[12]

Make sure people know what they are doing. Becoming a healthy evangelist involves understanding these five marks of conversion:

- Conversion itself is required.

- Conversion requires a clear understanding of the gospel.
- Conversion requires genuine faith.
- Conversion is followed by a changed life.
- Conversion results from God's action.

7

BE BOLD

Slaying the Fear Factor When Sharing Our Faith

Thabiti and I walked across the university courtyard. It was late; still darkness replaced the normal hustle and bustle of student campus life. It felt eerie to step from the bright lights, ornate auditorium and electric atmosphere of the Muslim-Christian dialogue into the warm desert night air of the Arabian Peninsula.

Thabiti had just spent five hours in dialogue and debate with Muslim friends. Thabiti sparkled; his warm, relaxed presence combined with his startling insight presented a powerful defense of the gospel as he challenged opinions, laid out facts, answered questions and proclaimed Christ.[1]

Bassam, our worthy Muslim opponent and friend, represented Islam. Bassam's deep understanding of the Bible and Christian theology would shame most Christians. He also understood some-thing else. As we left, Bassam gave me a hug and whispered in my ear, "One thing we agree about, Mack. We made history tonight." Bassam understood that Muslim-Christian dialogue just isn't done in the Arabian Peninsula.

When Thabiti and I reached the car parked in the sand lot be-hind the university, Thabiti leaned back in his seat, looked out my window and said the last thing I expected him to say: "Mack, since you called me to do this last year until the moment I stepped up to the mike, I have been afraid . . ."

Afraid? I had just watched my brother do one of the bravest things I'd ever seen with such grace and winsomeness that you would have thought that he was at a family picnic. Afraid? It was as if the three-camera film crew, reporters and photographers had been invited over for coffee in Thabiti's living room. Sure, some would believe that as a convert from Islam to Christianity, Thabiti should be executed (even Bassam believes converts who are citizens of Muslim nations should be executed), but Thabiti had never men-tioned it and we didn't talk about it much either . . . We all knew how very brave, how very bold Thabiti is with the gospel.

As I started the car, we both gazed at the moon peeking through one of the many scaffoldings surrounding yet another construc-tion site. "Thabiti, it only adds to the honor you gave to Christ tonight," I said, thinking of John 12:26.

Boldness is not a lack of fear. It is faith in something bigger than our fears so that we appear fearless. Confidence in something big-ger than our fears gives us the strength to do the right thing in spite of opposition or persecution.

If anything is needed in Christian witness today, it is boldness. We don't need bigger music ministries, longer prayer walks or nicer church foyers. We need boldness—wise boldness, gracious boldness, boldness rooted in the hope that we have in the gospel, boldness mixed with love, but boldness nonetheless.

Most Christians admire boldness in other people, and most Christians long for more boldness in their own lives. Boldness inspires us.

We sing, "Lord, magnify your name," which means we want God to be bigger in the hearts and minds of more people, but in reality our fears too often shrink God's name, as if we are looking at God through the wrong end of the telescope.

THE BASIC OBSTACLE TO BOLDNESS

So we must ask why we are timid. Why is it we desire to have the strength to face the raised fist yet can barely face the raised eyebrow? The basic obstacle to boldness is the fear of man. It's a plague and we have a bad case. Moreover, it's deadly to healthy evangelism.

The phrase "fear of man" comes from Proverbs 29:25: "Fear of man will prove to be a snare, / but whoever trusts in the LORD is kept safe." The fear of man is the fear that another person might expose, shame or harm you. And it's the greatest single obstacle to evangelism.[2] Fear of man replaces God and sets people as our chief end, our chief idol. Nowadays, rather than bending the knee to carved wood and metal idols, we bow to people, so much so that the fear of man has become the idolatry of our age.

There are many unhealthy ways to deal with the fear of man, which, in turn, become unhealthy evangelistic snares. We become people pleasers and so tell people what they want to hear. We shift blame and convince ourselves people won't listen. We tell ourselves that evangelism is too offensive. We run all the possible negative responses through our heads. The list goes on. By not dealing with our fear problem, we limit or distort evangelistic opportunities.

In high school, my newfound Christian faith propelled me to meet fellow Christians. That's how Mike Spencer became my friend. Nowadays I would say that he was discipling me, but that didn't really occur to either one of us then. His beat-up car served as the meeting place for prayer. It was a carbon monoxide death trap. I still remember bowing my head to pray and studying the asphalt of the school parking lot through the rusted-out floorboard. But Mike's passionate prayers are what really stuck in my mind: "God, if anyone needs to hear about your love, use us today to tell them the good news." Which at the time seemed about the dumbest, scariest thing in the world to pray. I had overwhelming teenage self-conscious "fear of man." It terrified me enough to think of some cool friend seeing me praying in the parking lot, let alone me evangelizing them.

But Mike's prayers for me made a difference. As I grew in the faith, I also grew in boldness. I needed prayer for boldness then, and I need prayers for boldness now. Our best response to fears is to pray, and get others to pray for us.

PAUL'S PRAYER REQUESTS

If ever there was a person who modeled boldness for the gospel, it was Paul, and Paul requested prayer for boldness more than anything else. Many books have been written about the prayers of Paul.[3] It is instructive to also look at the prayer *requests* of Paul, for in so doing we learn much about his bold heart.

84

Paul requests prayer in only five instances from four fellowships in the New Testament: the Romans, the Colossians, the Ephesians and the Thessalonians (twice). In those five instances there are twelve specific requests. A few of these are simply generic prayer requests: to the Thessalonians, for example, he just says, "pray for us" (1 Thessalonians 5:25). Or from the Romans he requests prayer (in 15:32) that God might make a way for him to visit the believers in Rome. It's notable that despite the withering attacks on Paul and the numerous hardships Paul faced, only twice does he ask for prayer for protection (Romans 15:31 and 2 Thessalonians 3:2).

His most frequent prayer request concerns the gospel and the spread of the gospel. When we think of Paul, this makes sense. He could barely write a sentence without making a beeline to the cross. So Paul asks that his fellow believers pray that the message of the gospel would "spread rapidly and be honored" (2 Thessalonians 3:1), for doors to open for the message, and when doors open, that he would be clear about the message (Colossians 4:3-4). In fact, he asks for prayer from the Ephesians (in 6:19) that *whenever* he opens his mouth the words of the gospel would be given to him.

Paul also asks for boldness in telling the good news. So he asks the Colossians for prayer that he will declare the gospel clearly, even when in chains (4:3-4). He tells the Ephesians (6:19-20) that his great desire is for boldness: "Pray also for me . . . that I will fearlessly make known the mystery of the gospel, for which I am an ambassador in chains. Pray that I may declare it fearlessly, as I should."

If Paul requests prayer to be fearless with the gospel, we should endeavor to gather prayers from others for ourselves. When was the last time you asked for prayer that you would be fearless with the gospel? We need others to pray that we would have opportunities to share, that when opportunities come we would be clear and have the right words, and most of all, that when we share we would be as fearless as Paul.

Healthy biblical knowledge helps us with our fear too. Look again at Proverbs 29:25. Here is the outline of our battle plan. The proverb contrasts the fear of man with trusting in the Lord. We overcome our fear of man by replacing it with something bigger—the trust of God. The writer is saying, in essence, don't make people your God; make God your God. Slay the idolatry of people. Put God in his rightful place.

In the New Testament we notice something similar that offers us three replacements for the fear of man. Jesus commands his followers to not be ashamed of him and his words, and he also says to fear God, who has the power of life after death (Luke 9:25-26; 12:5). So first we replace our fear of man with an understanding of God as judge.

Paul calls for boldness in his letters to Timothy and he points to the work of the Spirit within us (2 Timothy 1:7-8). So second, we replace any timidity by tapping into the Spirit's power.

Peter, who knew much about the fear of man (even a servant girl; see Mark 14:69-70), tells us, "Do not fear what they fear; do not be frightened," and then goes on to say, "but in your hearts set apart Christ as Lord" (1 Peter 3:14-15). Third, then, we replace our fears with heartfelt commitment to Christ's lordship.

In each of these New Testament passages we are told of something bigger than our fears: God as the ultimate judge, the Spirit of power within us and Christ the Lord of our hearts. This *is* the fear of the Lord which replaces the fear of man. All of these passages, unsurprisingly, deal with witness and evangelism, reminding us that God is bigger in our life.

When we place this proper fear of the Lord in our lives, notice three results. First, Paul says, "Since . . . we know what it is to fear the Lord, we try to persuade men" (2 Corinthians 5:11). Fear of the Lord results in healthy evangelism. When it slays our fears, it frees us to speak with our focus not on people, but on God (2 Corinthians 2:17).

Second, Paul says when we fear God rather than people, we become agents of reconciliation (2 Corinthians 5:11-20). Developing the proper fear of God is a critical key to produce bold healthy evangelism.

Finally, as we grow in boldness, we need to anticipate the places where boldness is required. To anticipate these situations for boldness is to be forearmed.

BOLDNESS IN CONVERSATION

I find three general areas where we need boldness over and over again in evangelistic efforts. First, we need boldness to simply expose our faith to others. Fear tends to isolate and compartmentalize our faith.

I'm not talking about buttonholing people in a conversation, but just simple, open honesty about our faith. Say a work colleague discovers you have a mutual friend. And in this particular conversation you have a choice about exposing your faith. You can say, "Oh, yes, I know Susan," and leave it at that. Or you can say, "Oh, yes, I know Susan. She's a friend of mine from church."

I would argue that the latter, though requiring a bit of boldness, is more honest and friendly. More importantly, it leaves a door open for the gospel. These small steps of boldness come upon us all the time, and often they shape our responses down the road to other opportunities requiring greater boldness. Anticipate situations where you can be honest with others about who you are as a person of faith.

The second area in which we need boldness is when the door is opened in actual conversation. This means acting in ways that show we are unashamed of the message we bear.

Leeann and I attended a formal dinner with a prominent businessman in Dubai. It was our first time to meet him. He is not a believer, though his wife is—and hence the invitation. Somewhere between hors d'oeuvres and the main course, the conversation turned toward issues of faith. There was banter between some of the guests, and then he turned and asked, "Mack, what do you think?"

I had a choice.

"Well, I tend not to kiss on the first date," I said, to chuckles around the table.

"Really, we want to know," he said.

"Well," I said, hesitating, but then plunging in, "there's bad news before there's good news, and the bad news is that we're rotten sinners. Were it not for God's mercy and love we would face certain destruction. We're under God's judgment right now. But the good news is that if we turn from our unbelief and pride and put our complete faith and trust in God's Son, believing that he has taken our sin on his body at the cross, and ask him for forgiveness as the risen Christ, we can enter into a restored relationship with the living God."

"Oh," he said. "Well, what about all the people who haven't heard? . . ."

And so it went until late into the night.

Now, nobody acted like the Philippian jailer and cried out, "What must I do to be saved?" But it takes some boldness to present the bald truth in a conversation . . . at a nice meal. Then we trust God to use it. Confront your own timidity and be willing to explain the message.

Finally, we need boldness to invite response to the message once we've presented it fully. This is overcoming the fear of rejection.

Perhaps you have been studying the Gospel of Mark with a non-Christian friend. There comes a point when you need boldness to say, "You know, I think that this is an urgent matter in your life. I think that you understand the gospel, and really what is left is for you to place your complete faith and trust in Christ. What is stopping you from doing that?"

We tend to hate putting people on the spot, but the gospel is not really the gospel without letting people know that a response is required.

So remember: to be healthy evangelists requires boldness that overcomes the fear of man by replacing it with the fear of God. Healthy evangelism is cultivated by exposing our faith to others, by anticipating how to be bold in our conversations and by being willing to invite a response to the message.

As I put the finishing touches on the last paragraphs for this chapter, the phone rang.

"Could you receive some friends passing through town?" They didn't have much time but they wanted to see me.

We sat in the living room. "Ben and Sarah," a young married couple, had just spent three months under house arrest and daily interrogation from the secret police simply because they are Christian leaders in their country. Now they were fleeing. The secret police did not physically harm them, and for that we were grateful, but it was three months of abusive threats and tactics of fear ending with deportation.

In a matter of a couple days they had become refugees. Now, just off the plane, they were filled with questions and uncertainty. Their story poured out between bouts of quiet weeping. The tremendous toll the interrogation took showed in their slumped shoulders; gone were the happy spirits that marked them a few short months before. Their eyes darted back and forth; sleep had proved elusive they said. At one point Ben put his head in his hands and said, "I've lost everything: my country, my family, my church, but I have Jesus and he is worth it. He's the one we live for."

When we prayed together, Ben prayed for his interrogator, and he prayed that the message he had shared with that man would lead him to faith—the message Ben had given him *under interrogation*. Ben's bold witness seemed straight out of the book of Acts. The connection to Paul's desire for bold witness, though chained and in jail, was uncanny. I'm humbled when I compare my fears with Ben's boldness. It's good to remember what much of the world faces when we think of our fears.

Ben said it was awful, but he now knows what it is to suffer for Jesus, and he told me, "Write this in your book. . . . Tell them to be bold."

Worldly Love and Its Fruits

Mistaking the World's Love for God's Love

I love Aunt Sue. A retired elementary school teacher, Aunt Sue's personality is filled with sweetness. Besides, she's a fan of my books.

Recently she asked me what I thought about a popular Christian book on the *New York Times* Bestseller List. I said I felt suspicious of any book, short of the Bible, appearing on the *New York Times* Bestseller List.

"Broad popularity really isn't compatible with selling biblical books," I said as I rubbed my chin, wondering if Aunt Sue could tell I was secretly jealous.

Aunt Sue seemed to grow much taller than her diminutive four-foot-eleven-inch frame. She fixed her eyes on me, and suddenly I knew how this dear woman kept order in her classroom.

She spoke not to a married man who is the father of three grown sons but to a very naughty young man.

"Mack," she said sternly, "that book is about God's love, and it's wonderful!" Her eyes got squinty as she peered over her glasses at me. "Have you read it?"

"Oh, well, no, I'll have to get it . . ." I stammered, back-peddling, realizing she had nailed me. I had just criticized a book I hadn't read, and I dissed the love of God.

If there is anything anyone knows about Christianity, it's that God is love, right? What else could raise such ire from sweet Aunt Sue?

And it's true. God is love.

The apostle John writes of Christ's love as an eyewitness. When John wrote, "God is love" (1 John 4:16), it came with memories of walking side by side with the Lord of love, listening to the teachings of love, watching love's greatest action as Christ hung on the cross.

It's not merely true. It's a profound culture-shaping revelation. In the first century, values such as nobility, honor and power carried more weight than the weak value of love. But crystallized in one verse, 1 John 4:16, this idea changed culture for millenniums to come. Now even those from remote Christian backgrounds believe that love is the highest of godly virtues and values.

When we compare Christian love to other religions, we see what a unique treasure Christian love is. Love is merely one of the ninety-nine names of Allah in Islam.[1] It's not mentioned in the eightfold path of Buddhism.[2] It's remote and distant for Hindus and usually more tied to sex. It's only Christianity that holds "God is love."

So what's the love problem for evangelism? It's a distinguishing mark of Christianity, and it's certainly a place where both Christians and non-Christians agree. What could be a clearer Christian mandate for healthy evangelism than love? Doesn't Paul say that when we think of evangelism we act because "Christ's love compels us" (2 Corinthians 5:14)?

Yes, of course, love should mark every part of our evangelism. And the Christian community has done a good job teaching about God's love. But here's the concern: if we only speak of God's love while forsaking God's other attributes (such as holiness, righteousness and justice), we are tailoring God to a popular image, an idol really, and not the God of the Bible.

The lenses of culture distort the concept of love. As a result, the love popularly ascribed to God is often not truly biblical love. When we speak to the culture about God's love, we need to be sure we're talking about the same thing.

What I want to say to Aunt Sue is, "Yes, we all love the love of God, but many use the popular culture's view of God's love to sell books and fill huge auditoriums. But they present a misshapen view of God." Unsurprisingly, this results in unhealthy evangelism.

So let's identify three primary ways the biblical view of God's love differs from that in pop culture and trace how these misunderstandings bleed into Christian thought and into unhealthy evangelism.

1. Pop Culture Believes God's Love Is Sentimental

Sentimental love is gushy and focused on feelings. Sentimental love sacrifices truth. In fact, sentimental love is often used to justify unloving actions based on feelings. Take the pop song "(If Loving You Is Wrong) I Don't Want to Be Right,"[3] a song justifying adultery based on a rush of feelings.

Sentimental love mimics compassion. But it's as silly as sending a Hallmark card to a village of starving people in Darfur hoping they'll get better.

Sentimental love bleeds into the Christian mind in a form of niceness. It's easy to confuse nice with compassion, kindness or love. But *nice* is not a biblical word. Jesus was extremely un-nice at times, because he wanted to go deeply into people's lives, into their sin with the truth, and that's never nice.

Ultimately, sentimental love trivializes love, and it trivializes evangelism. Pop culture says it's not nice to talk about religious convictions. The healthy evangelist is willing to push, lovingly, against the tide of pop thinking and speak truth into people's lives. Remember there is nothing sentimental or gushy about God's love. Sentimental love becomes very weak in the face of real difficulties, while true biblical love is hard as nails. It's the love of the cross that took seriously our predicament and our potential, and provided a solution far better than a good feeling. Healthy evangelism speaks the truth in love (Ephesians 4:15).

D. A. Carson tells us to beware of sentimental pop views of love: "To love wisely and well, to love appropriately, to love faithfully, to love in line with biblical expectations . . . is commonly a very difficult thing to do."[4]

2. POP CULTURE BELIEVES GOD'S LOVE
IS UNIVERSAL AND UNCONDITIONAL

Pop culture believes God loves us unconditionally in a way that means we are all fine just the way we are. This love requires no change or commitment. This is the kind of love that believes that true love lets anyone do anything they want.

This kind of love mimics the freedom Christ offers but leaves out the step of repenting and believing. So it's compulsory heaven for everyone, no matter what you've done or what you believe—and never mind about God bringing justice to the world.

Unfortunately, this pop understanding of God's unconditional love fills the church. Certainly, the Bible talks of unconditional love, but not all expressions of God's love are unconditional. That is, God doesn't love only one way.[5] God loves both unconditionally *and* conditionally. For instance, God pours out his love on his creation—unconditionally. Jesus said that the rain falls on the righteous and the unrighteous (Matthew 5:45). This is his unconditional, providential love.

In other cases God loves conditionally. For example, John says, "To all who received him, to those who believed in his name, he gave the right to become children of God" (John 1:12). This is a clear condition: you must receive him; then he will give you the right to be a child of God—freely, wonderfully, full of grace and mercy, but on the condition that you receive him for who he says he is. His saving love is conditional. Conditional love is not second-rate love. It's how God chooses to love for that context.

The problems start when Christians begin communicating God's providential love (for everyone, unconditionally) as if it's God's saving love (not for everyone and conditional). Because the world sees God's love as universal, there appears to be no need to commit or repent since "he loves us just the way we are."

When Christians get this mixed up they scramble the message.

Years ago it was common to hear, "God loves you and has a

wonderful plan for your life." Yes, God is "providentially" with-holding his judgment from you and thereby showing you his un-conditional love. But to promise a wonderful plan without clearly explaining God's condition, to repent of sin, for example, violates the clear teachings of the Bible.

The challenge for healthy evangelism? Whereas sentimental love's bland "niceness" works against truth, unconditional love re-jects the call of God to commit, or repent. So remember, when we speak of God's love, especially about salvation, we are speaking about God's conditions to produce changed hearts.[6]

Where sentimental love trivializes love, pop unconditional love trivializes sin, as if God winks at sin. Don't treat sin, John Owens says, "as a naughty child, but loved." Remember God hates sin in all of its forms.

Furthermore, keep in mind that Jesus makes an exclusive claim. Jesus said he is *the* truth (John 14:6). His terms are that we must come to our senses, be aware of our sin, understand the gospel and turn to Christ in faith—these are God's conditions to receive the benefits of his love. So never forget to call people to move into a relationship with God on his terms, his conditions, not ours.

3. Pop Culture Believes That God's Love Is Me-Centered

Me-centered love is a modern-day love tsunami. It's all about me. A culture that believes that God exists to satisfy my personal de-sires soon loses an ability to sacrifice for God and others. Where sentimental love gives up truth, and universal love gives up justice, me-centered love gives up sacrifice. Me-centered love so twists the meaning of love, it's actually a synonym for selfish sin. Me-centered love yearns to indulge insatiable desires.

Me-centered love easily bleeds into Christian thinking about God's love. We start thinking God's love is about my world and me. We start treating God as a celestial butler, and singing songs that make it hard to tell if Jesus is a savior or a boyfriend. Take this refrain for instance: "Like a rose, trampled on the ground, / You took the fall and thought of me; / Above all."[7]

This song about Christ's crucifixion is wildly popular. But contrast the words of Christ as he approached his crucifixion: "Now my heart is troubled, and what shall I say? 'Father, save me from this hour'? No, it was for this very reason I came to this hour. Father, glorify your name!" (John 12:27-28).[8]

Jesus *above all* desired for the Father to be glorified. He was not thinking of me above the Father. He was not thinking of me more than another person, for that matter. Doesn't this song point to our Western privatized selfishness? Yet, Christians by the thousands sing this song and never realize its message is more culture than Bible. Unfortunately this song reinforces a worldly concept that the love of God is focused on me.

Me-centered love is a particular challenge to healthy evangelism. We are tempted to offer a me-centered message of a God who will indulge our desires—after all, it gets results . . . by the millions. It packs people into auditoriums and rockets books to the top of the *New York Times* Bestseller List, but what is offered is a grossly distorted mix of Santa and Baal, which is crucifying the message of the gospel. It is another gospel (Galatians 1:7-9).

The healthy evangelist must avoid this temptation at all costs.

Our message is not me-centered but cross-centered. Jesus said, "If anyone would come after me, he must deny himself and take up his cross and follow me. For whoever wants to save his life will lose it, but whoever loses his life for me will find it" (Matthew 16:24-25).

Understand that the call to a cross is a call to crucify our desire to be the center of the universe. This is a call to love sacrificially. To be a healthy evangelist you must stand against me-centered love by demonstrating self-sacrificing love.

One of the best ways to show self-sacrificing love is to share your faith; it's a part of picking up the cross. Especially when you share your faith in the face of a hostile culture. To understand that self-sacrificing love is our motivation in evangelism is at the very heart of healthy evangelism.

Missionary Jack Miller didn't just talk about biblical love, he practiced it. During the last years of his life he waged battles with an unhealthy body: cancer, strokes and a weak heart. As he traded his pulpit for a hospital bed, hospital rooms became places of love and witness, as patients, hospital staff and doctors heard of the message of the gospel. In some hospitals sick patients embraced the gospel. An entire church formed out of the hospital staff after one stay in a Ugandan clinic.[9]

As he grew weaker, his love grew stronger. Where most would have given up and focused on themselves, he kept giving. He knew others were in greater peril than he himself was. Consider the title of his last sermon, "A Dying Man Preaching to Dying Men." That's what loving, healthy evangelism is all about.

Jack died in Spain after heart surgery. He never left the ICU, but Jack Miller's example left a legacy of loving, healthy evangelism that will far outlive him.

Reject sentimentality's cheap imitation of love. Embrace a love that takes people seriously, the kind of love earthy enough to get into a grave for us. Speak into lives with truth and grace.

Expand God's love beyond the clichés of universal love. Do not fear a love that sets God's conditions plainly for all to see; to do otherwise is unloving. Speak of the exclusiveness of Christ's love.

Move from a love that is self-indulgent to a cross-centered, self-sacrificing love—a love that is in line with the message we share. Demonstrate love with the sacrifice of your life.

In so doing people will see the real love of God, and you will be a healthy evangelist.

Love among God's people plays a special part in healthy evangelism—the subject of our next chapter.

9

THE GOSPEL MADE VISIBLE

The Church

The bride hailed from Baghdad, the groom from Pittsburgh. At the end of the service I pronounced my short homily, and Pastor Onsy, of the Arab Church, pronounced them man and wife. They exited, and Onsy invited the gathering to a lavish sit-down reception in the adjacent room. A hungry crowd surged toward the door; it had been a three-hour wedding which had started an hour late.

But there was plenty of food at the reception and singing, dancing and clapping. I shouted greetings to a young couple at my table; she was from Brazil and he was from Lebanon.

"Do you attend church here?" I asked.

"Yes," he said, "we do."

"I don't think we've met," I said.

"Well, actually, we attend all churches."

"Really," I said, "how do you do that?"

"Well, we simply go to all the churches. Right now we are attending the Indian church." He waved his hand toward the congregation that was meeting across the way.

"We're all a part of the same body," he added. He seemed a bit defensive.

"Well, yes," I said, not really knowing what to say, "that's, uh, true . . ."

"It's very beneficial for us," he said. The woman nodded her agreement. "When we're bored we simply move on. So church is always fresh."

"We love how colorful they are," she said. I think she was talking about the Indian church.

"I see," I said, ". . . and besides that, you're never around long enough to have any messy disagreements."

"Precisely!" he responded, missing my shot at irony.

My, oh, my . . . how do I unpack that? I wondered. "Please, pass the olives," was the best I could do.

That twenty-five-second conversation seems to represent our entire generation's sad theology about the church: that the church is for our personal benefit; that the main requirement of church is for it to be fresh, colorful and entertaining; that church relationships are secondary, even disposable; and that the church is more about consumerism than relationship.

But if you want to be a healthy evangelist you must demonstrate a healthy love for the church. Nobody is surprised when evangelism is linked with loving others, but what is surprising to many is the strong link Jesus makes between evangelism and love for the church. That's because the church does not exist as a way to fulfill us; it demonstrates the truth of Christ to a watching world.

And that *is* worth unpacking.

LOVING OTHER CHRISTIANS AND EVANGELISM

On the eve of his death Jesus said, "A new command I give you: Love one another" (John 13:34). This is by far the most important command for healthy evangelism. We are to love the church.

This love we have for the body of believers is distinct. While we are to love all people, this is a special love for those found in Christ. Which only makes sense. When we come together with other believers, we share the deepest, most intimate spiritual connection we could possibly share—salvation in Christ.

I've worshiped with believers around the world: Masai warriors in Kenya, Ixil farmers in Guatemala, university students in Korea and Arab businessmen in Dubai. They didn't speak my language; they didn't know my culture and none of them worshiped God in a manner I found familiar. Yet the communion with them was greater than any connection I would have with a person who speaks my language and comes from my culture, but who doesn't know God.

In that regard, the young couple I spoke to at the wedding reception is correct. We are a part of one body. But there's more to our love for Christ's body than merely sampling church. They were missing something very important.

Look carefully at the biblical text from John. "A new command I give you: Love one another. As I have loved you, so you must love one another. By this all men will know that you are my disciples, if you love one another" (John 13:34-35). Notice the love is costly. Jesus says that our love in community is a "as I have loved you" love. We love each other after the pattern of Jesus. Or, as Mark Dever says, the shape of "the true church is cruciform."[1] That is, love which looks like the cross is shaped by the sacrifice of the cross. This is far from flitting from fellowship to fellowship.

But also notice the condition that Jesus sets: that *if* we love, *then* all men will know we are Christ's disciples. The sobering thing about this condition is that Jesus is giving a watching world the right to say that if we do not love one another, the world can rightly conclude we are not his disciples.[2] So it is clear that this love must be *seen* by the world, not just felt by believers.

There is a parallel passage concerning a watching world later in John: "My prayer is not for them alone. I pray also for those who will believe in me through their message, that all of them may be one, Father, just as you are in me and I am in you. May they also be in us so that the world may believe that you have sent me" (John 17:20-21).

Notice the prayer is first for oneness or unity between believers. Jesus prays that this oneness would be like the oneness of Jesus and God the Father. And second, the prayer is that these unified believers would be one with Christ and God the Father. And again, notice the condition Jesus sets. That *if* we are united with one another and with Christ, *then* the watching world may believe that God the Father has sent Jesus.

Is there any clearer instruction from Jesus about evangelism than when he prayed this prayer for his disciples and for us?

Do we get that? For all the work that is put into evangelistic outreach and all the training that goes into personal evangelism and the method of evangelism, for all the books that are written about apologetics, Jesus commissions genuine believers to exhibit Godlike unity so that the world may believe that God sent Jesus.

It's important to point out that Jesus is not praying for mystic sweet communion alone. That's because both our love and our unity are visible to the watching world. Neither is this mere organizational cooperation; that goes on but in a way that is devoid of love with disappointing regularity. No, both the love of John 13 and the unity of John 17 must be observed; it is demonstrable love and demonstrable unity between genuine believers before a watching world.

How odd, one might say, that the best way to demonstrate that Jesus is from the Father and that we are his followers is not through method or technique or apologetics. It's through loving, unified community among believers. As Francis Schaeffer says:

> Our love will not be perfect, but it must be substantial enough for the world to be able to observe or it does not fit into the structure of the verses in John 13 and 17. And if the world does not observe this among true Christians, the world has a right to make the two awful judgments which these verses indicate: That we are not Christians and that Christ was not sent by the Father.[3]

"The world will know I am from the Father by your love one for another." This seems counterintuitive to healthy evangelism. Wouldn't it make far more sense to say that if we are to be healthy evangelists we need to just tell people about the gospel—never mind this business about the church? Well, certainly it's true we need to proclaim the gospel to people. But as Mark Dever says, "Christian proclamation might make the gospel audible, but Christians living together in local congregations make the gospel visible. The church is the gospel made visible."[4]

And since the church is the gospel made visible it makes sense for Christians who have any concern for evangelism to be very careful to love the church.

Jesus said that if you do not love the church of Christ you are in danger of proving to the world that Jesus is not the Son of God. Again Francis Schaeffer says,

> So, we are to love all true Christian brothers in a way that the world may observe. This means showing love to our brother in the midst of our differences—great or small— loving our brothers when it costs us something, loving them even under times of tremendous emotional tension, loving them in a way the world can see. In short, we are to practice and exhibit the holiness of God and the love of God, for without this we grieve the Holy Spirit.
>
> Love—and the unity it attests to—is the mark Christ gave Christians to *wear* before the world. Only with this mark may the world know that Christians are indeed Christians and that Jesus was sent by the Father.[5]

So, the method of evangelism that Jesus institutes is unity and love among believers. Yet how often I meet would-be evangelists who don't love the church; to paraphrase, they love the church in general, but no church specifically.

How do we wear the mark of love before the watching world? How do we make the shape of our community cruciform? These are radical questions, and they require a radical response.

What follows is a list of radical, mind-blowing, evangelism-producing principles that, if practiced, will change the world. You have fair warning—these are countercultural, even bizarre to the watching world, but they demonstrate love for one another.

16 Ways to Demonstrate Love and Unity in the Church and in So Doing Become a Healthy Evangelist

1. Attend a church that takes the gospel seriously (Hebrews 10:25). Treat form as secondary, the gospel as primary. Incense and candles, rock band worship, liturgy, Gregorian chants, a pastor with tattoos . . . these are "form" and therefore secondary. Clear gospel proclamation from the leadership is primary.[6]

2. Become an actual member of a church. I'm serious; membership shows your loving commitment to one another.[7] This is truly radical. Go against the grain and show that you are really crazy in love with Jesus and join a church. And just think, the less cool the church the more opportunity to demonstrate real love!

3. Read C. J. Mahaney's book *Humility* once a year.[8] This book is a powerhouse of practical help for anyone who desires to be great in the kingdom of God. Mahaney gives us practical tools for demonstrating love and unity in the context of community.

4. Turn down jobs that might take you away from church even if they pay more.

5. Arrange family vacations around your church's schedule. Or better yet, take your family on a short-term mission trip with other members instead of a family vacation. This will blow people's minds.

6. If your church doesn't have a church covenant, think about developing one that expresses your love for each other.[9]

7. Move to a house closer to the church and use your house as a place of hospitality (Romans 12:13).

8. Practice church discipline. It's biblical (Matthew 18:15-17). This is truly, off-the-charts radical. Church discipline is not usually what people think it is; the goal of church discipline is always to restore, not to punish. You may offend people, but then again you may save some from living a hell on earth.[10]

9. Respect, even revere, the authority in the church (1 Thessalonians 5:12-13).

10. Turn heads—really practice the biblical teachings of giving and receiving forgiveness. Be quick to forgive others (Ephesians 4:32). Be quick to say you're sorry (Matthew 5:23-24). Forgiveness may be one of the most radical ways to express love and unity in a congregation, and it's rarely practiced.[11]

11. Take care of people who are in need physically in your congregation (Romans 12:13).

12. Pray for each other (Ephesians 6:18). Don't just say you'll pray. Actually put into place some ways to pray for each and every member.

13. Sympathize with other believers (Romans 12:15). Check a critical spirit.

14. Focus on caring for one another spiritually by discipling one another (Galatians 6:1-2). Though discipling only looks like having lunch, it's secretly and subversively radical. Over a Caesar salad ask the dangerous question: "How're things spiritually?"

15. Share your faith together (Philippians 1:27). A loving church committed to each other will see the Lord add to their numbers (Acts 2:42-47). Involve your friends at church with your evangelistic efforts.

16. Read Mark Dever's *9 Marks of a Healthy Church*.

Okay, so maybe this list isn't the kind of radical thinking that would land you on the Homeland Security watch list, but in the spiritual realm it's as radical as it gets. And this kind of radical love leads to radical evangelism.

To be a healthy evangelist means to love brothers and sisters. This is a spiritual reality that has huge ramifications, so if you have any desire to be a healthy evangelist, move beyond thinking of our Christian community as a self-help tool and move toward what Jesus desires in Christian community: observable love and unity among true believers.

10

A Manifesto for Healthy Evangelism

Taking Action

I drove north and east along Sheik Zayed Highway to the Dubai airport. My mission: to drop off a load of kids for the youth group's short-term trip to India. My thoughts ranged between the shape of the church in Bangalore to the shape of a passing Ferrari, which made me wonder if my car stood still. My thoughts were interrupted when Leah, the perkiest of the perky Parks girls, piped up, "Uncle Mack,[1] you're writing a book on evangelism, right?"

Here's my chance, I thought. Though Leah is unusually bright, if I could explain the book to a thirteen-year-old, then I could get the concept across to anyone.

"Well, not exactly, Leah," I said. "I've already written a book about evangelism."

"Yeah," she said, "*Speaking of Jesus.*"

(I love Leah.) "Right," I said. "So this book is a bit different. I'm trying to write a book about basic ideas that make up healthy evangelism before we ever share our faith."

"Oh, that makes sense," said Leah.

Maybe she's too bright, I thought. But for the rest of us . . .

A MANIFESTO FOR HEALTHY EVANGELISM

- Healthy evangelism is rooted in our own commitment of faith in Christ rather than in any pragmatic method of evangelism. So, first, we become people of faith by putting our complete trust and faith in Jesus. Since we trust with our whole lives that the gospel is true, we desire to share the gospel out of faithfulness, not technique.

- We become students of the gospel. We know it through and through. We resist the natural tendency to shape the gospel to our personal tastes and the tastes of the culture by adding to or subtracting from the message.

- The healthy evangelist guards the gospel. Because we know that the gospel can be lost, we never assume the gospel but emphasize the gospel in our fellowships and in Christian leadership.

- The first application of our understanding of the gospel is not necessarily to share our faith, but to live a gospel-centered life. So we sit at the foot of the cross when there are differences with other brothers and sisters. We remember our own sin and failings when we discipline our children. We apply principles of grace in our marriage and with our coworkers. We especially think through how gospel themes bear on our presentations of the gospel to make sure the message we bear looks like the message we share.

- We always remember that evangelism is an act of social action and produces social change in and of itself. It is not a category separate from social action.

- Since many things mimic true Christian conversion, we gain a clear biblical understanding of conversion. The healthy evangelist knows that the hearer must understand the message of the gospel before conversion can happen. True conversion, when it does happen, is marked by a radically changed life. We understand that we're only instruments in the hands of God, that God is the one who generates conversion.

- The healthy evangelist seeks boldness in witness and works to slay the "fear of man," one of the great obstacles to sharing faith.

- Since love is the mark of a Christian, we endeavor to gain a biblical view of love, while rejecting corrosive, worldly views of love.

- The healthy evangelist knows, in the light of the commands of Jesus in John 13 and John 17, that biblical love, practically applied in the church, is the greatest image of the gospel we offer the world.

- As we speak the gospel to those who don't know the gospel, we cycle through three foundational challenges in our minds: Do I know the gospel? Do I live the gospel? Do I speak the gospel?

It's not essential to follow this manifesto point by point. There are thousands of stories of how people did goofy things to share their faith and even more of people actually coming to faith in the strangest ways. We shouldn't be surprised that people come to faith in bizarre ways. God can hit straight with a crooked stick, it's been said.

But goofiness in evangelism can have dangerous results if it's used to justify bad practice. The bad practice is what must stop, for the sake of the church. Bad evangelistic practices, promoted simply because God is gracious to an individual, form bad discipleship and bring about the statistics we saw in chapter one about Christian hypocrisy. Turn the tide by practicing healthy gospel-centered evangelism, which produces gospel-centered disciples.

Start by getting the principles of the manifesto[2] fixed in your mind. In so doing you will become who you are meant to be.

TAKE ACTION

We must also take action. Yes, take action. The fact is, we *can't* be healthy evangelists if we don't take action. Sometimes we can spend so much time studying evangelism that we never do evangelism, but the time is short, and it's easy to get stuck. So here are some ideas that are helpful in taking action in evangelism.

Body check. Do a body check to see if anything is holding you back. Check your head—is the gospel on your mind as you go through your day? Check your gut—are you willing to be bold with the gospel in the face of fears? Check your feet—are you willing to move out in a hostile world and speak the truth?

Pray. Start by praying for those you know who don't know Christ. Maybe it's a family member or a coworker or a friend or a friend of a friend. Pray for them regularly. Remember that praying for others will make you more attuned to Spirit-led opportunities. I've noticed how often I get to share with people for whom I'm praying. Imagine that!

If they are open, pray for them when you are together too. Recently, during a time of unrest in Iran, two Iranian friends called us. They had previously felt touched with how we prayed personally for others. That was new to them, and they wanted prayers for themselves and their country. Of course we were thrilled but we did one better. We invited these Muslim friends to a time of prayer for Iran. They were happy to join us. So we gathered some Christians together and prayed for Iran and the safety of their families. But we prayed the gospel for them too. In some contexts Muslims may have taken offense, but in this context they were touched and moved, their hearts open to hearing more about the work of Christ.

Plan. It's good to think through settings where you might be able to share your faith. Do you have a trip coming up? Will you be on a school field trip? Are you greeting new people at church? I find that often the biggest obstacle to evangelism is a mental block to sharing. Make sure the gospel is on your heart and that you are open to God opening doors for you.

Maybe you are in a pattern where you just don't see people anymore. So ready your heart to be used by God and God will use you.

Think. Think through issues. Jesus answered the woman at the well. Much of Paul's ministry was to sweep away objections. How do we cultivate Paul's attitude to do anything needed for the gospel? We need to do some work here. Be ready to deal with clichés about Christianity that others may have never thought through adequately.

Think though those things which are obstacles. Do some study. Never use apologetics to win an argument, but do use them to deal with genuine objections to faith. Actually, a tremendous benefit to apologetics is to make a (gentle) statement that you are not unaware of that problem, that you have not kissed your brains goodbye, but that you are still a person of faith.

Prepare. Practice the "gospel in a minute." Know how to say the basic principles of the gospel message in a minute or two. I use "God, Man, Christ, Response" as an outline in my head. But the basic principle is to think through what needs to be communicated so that someone can understand what God has done through Christ for lost sinners such as us, so that we might repent of our sins and turn to Christ in faith.[3] Say it in language you would use naturally in conversation with friends.

Pastors, get your congregation equipped with the gospel. By training your congregation to share their faith in everyday situations, you will have a far bigger audience in the world than you could ever have at church.

All of us should be ready for openings for the gospel that are out of the blue. Don't get stuck thinking that God only uses us to share in one kind of place. I've noticed that when I'm thinking about sharing my faith with specific people, I usually end up witnessing to other people too. When we have the gospel on our hearts the Lord is going to use us.

Get started. Have a hobby or activity you enjoy? Connect with other like-minded people if you don't already. Have lunch with people. If you are a more mature Christian, hang out with new believers; not only do they usually know many nonbelievers, but also the time with them can be used to help them grow in the faith.

Be bold in conversation as was discussed in chapter seven. Ask spiritual questions: "What spiritual interests do you have?" "What is your faith background?" These are good neutral questions you can ask. Spiritual issues are often topics of conversations and on people's minds. There's no offense in asking people questions about what they think. Take them seriously, listen, probe, figure out the logic of their thoughts. Keep asking questions until they ask you some questions.

Be on the lookout to share in places where it isn't so hard. Not everyone is a foaming-at-the-mouth atheist. Sometimes the best place is in church—visitors and friends of new members obviously have some spiritual interest or they wouldn't be there. What could be more natural in conversation?

Gather. Unfortunately events are often the first thing we think of when we think of evangelism, but they tend to be the least effective. Still, events are helpful discussion starters and can be an easy way to sort through who is interested and who isn't. There are many creative ways to gather people together to talk over spiritual issues. The best is on their turf.

Start a prayer group or a home Bible study. Often people who would never darken the door of a church are interested in a home group—maybe your next-door neighbor.

My favorite thing to do is study the Scripture with people. Read the text and see what people say. You don't need to go to seminary to lead some people through a passage in the book of Mark. If someone asks a genuine question and you don't know the answer say, "I don't know." But find out and have an answer for them later. Try to have the study at a neutral site. I gathered a group of very committed Muslim guys together who were some of the best Bible study members I've ever had. They took the text seriously, they loved looking at the Scripture, they liked how the Bible is logical and practical, and besides, they are instructed by the Qur'an to read the gospel (something I made sure to point out).

If you are blessed with a church that is faithfully presenting the message of the gospel week after week, then take your friends to your church.

Serve. Practice service to those around you. The community in which you live needs to be loved. Living a redemptive life of service points to a God who redeems. Put into practice the command by Peter to "live such good lives among the pagans that, though they accuse you of doing wrong, they may see your good deeds and glorify God on the day he visits us" (1 Peter 2:12). Pray for the good of the people around you. Find ways to contribute to the good of the community around you.

Speak. Have a heart that is ready to turn conversations to Christ—not by manipulation but, when a spiritual issue comes up, by pausing and thinking through a way to respond graciously that at least opens the door for a thought about Jesus.

Try to speak of Jesus. Don't spend much time on the Spanish Inquisition. Focus on Jesus; he is the most intriguing person ever. The story of Christ is more compelling than this month's movie blockbuster, and most people don't know the story.[4]

Pursue. Don't give up. Be persistent with people. My friend

Frank tells how his entire family came to Christ because his daughter shared the gospel with him and his wife. She had come to faith on campus through the constant pursuit of Brian, my coworker.

Invite. Finally, don't forget to invite people to cross the line into a relationship with the living Christ. Many are just waiting for someone to tell them what the next step of faith is for their lives . . .

THE PRIVILEGE IS OURS

The sermon was finished and, in closing, Pastor Daniel reminded us to share our faith. For some reason it pierced me. I've been walking with Jesus for thirty years, and I still feel like evangelism is rolling the ball uphill. Even so, I felt compelled to turn to the two Filipino women on my left, thinking that they might not know the Lord. After chatting a moment it became clear that they actually were vibrant believers. Undaunted, I stood up and talked to a young couple from Sri Lanka I had not seen before. Not only were they Christians, but they were also leaders in Ajith Fernando's church in Colombo.

No, not them, I thought.

By this time, Manglaran, the church custodian, had half of the chairs together in the middle of the room, formally a dining room that had been cleared out to serve us as our house church. I turned to walk around a tall stack of brown plastic chairs, and I practically ran over a thin young man standing next to the chairs. He looked about the age of my oldest son.

"Hello," he said, "can you help me?"

"Yes," I said. And I just knew. In some strange way, I knew he was the one I had been looking for.

He held a worn Bible in his hand.

"My name's Mack," I said, sticking out my hand. "How can I be of service?" I asked.

"My name is Basanta." He took my hand and held on to it.

"Ba-san-ta," I repeated.

"Yes," he said, "Basanta."

Though later his name would roll off my tongue, "Basanta" was a name I needed to repeat slowly. "I'm glad to meet you, Ba-san-ta," I said. He was still holding my hand.

"I'm from Nepal."

"Oh," I said, trying to remember the religion of Nepal. Not Christian; I knew that. *Hindu?* I thought to myself. Almost everyone had gone from the villa, but I asked Manglaran to leave two chairs out for us to talk. Basanta and I sat in the middle of the empty room.

Without any other word he said, "Can you tell me how to become a Christian?"

"Yes, I can," I responded as if this happened all the time.

And so I began to explain the message of faith. "Through one man sin has come to us all; his name was Adam . . ." The gospel is an amazingly universal message.

I got out a piece of paper and sketched out the gospel. I spoke slowly and distinctly, and I went over key concepts of the gospel: God, Man, Christ, Response. Basanta seemed rapt (and he still has that piece of paper). I asked if he understood. His English was good, but still it was clear that English was his second language. We took as much time as it took to exhaust his questions. I asked him if he was ready to turn his life over to Christ.

"Yes, I am ready," he said, "but I have a story that I want to tell you before I do."

"Okay," I said.

"You see this Bible?" he said.

"Yes," I said.

"My brother works in Saudi Arabia. Someone gave him this Bible, and he became a Christian," he said.

Wow, they don't have many Bibles in Saudi. That's amazing, I thought to myself.

"And so he sent this Bible to my other brother who works in Iraq. He is a driver there in a very dangerous place, and he became a Christian too."

Basanta placed the Bible in my hands and continued. "He sent this Bible on to my mother and my father in Nepal, and they became Christians. Now they have a church meeting in their house."

Oh my word, I thought. I had just landed in the middle of a family revival. I turned the Bible over in my hands.

Basanta continued, ". . . and I am the last brother. My parents sent me the Bible, and they have all told me that I must become a Christian too. So I am here to become a Christian."

I think my mouth hung open. "Basanta, that's the most amazing story I have ever heard," I said, caressing his Bible and wondering how it got to Saudi, and thinking that some Christian out there had no idea that it was having an impact from the Arabian Peninsula to Nepal. Never underestimate the power of God's Word.

I listened to Basanta give his life to Jesus in that empty villa. In some ways it happened naturally. In another way it seemed bizarre and supernatural. When I went home that night and tried to describe it to the family, it seemed unreal. I wasn't really sure it had happened. But it had.

Basanta kept coming to church. We started studying the Scripture together. He was raised Hindu, and in our first study—on the Ten Commandments—Basanta was shocked to discover "no more idols." But as a result, he threw them away—his first radical act of discipleship. My son, Tristan, began to meet weekly with Basanta to go over the Bible. Later I had the delight of talking to his brother in Saudi over the phone. At his baptism, Basanta again told his story about his journey of faith and how it included a Bible, some faithful family members and me. Me! What joy!

I am fully convinced that if I had not run into Basanta behind those plastic chairs, God would have made sure some other Christian with the gospel on their heart would have, but I am so grateful that I didn't miss the opportunity.

That's the best part of healthy evangelism—when the opportunities become bigger than the obstacles. For me, the greatest point of healthy evangelism is when we gain a picture of just what it is that we're a part of. Evangelism is not a duty to perform; it's not a cross we must bear. It's a privilege we're granted.

The privilege is ours. The greatest thing about evangelism is that we get to do it—you and me. Somehow the great Creator God allows us—protoplasmic specks in the universe—to partner with him in his grand design. It's a wonder and a mystery. To be healthy—really healthy—not just in evangelism, but in all of our spiritual life, is to have just a glimpse of what it means to take hold of that privilege in faith, with truth, through love, and in boldness and faithfulness to the praise of his glorious grace.

BE IN TOUCH

Please write me with thoughts, comments and questions:

mackstiles@gmail.com

NOTES

Chapter 1. Roger's Question: *Don't Peddle the Gospel*

[1] All Scripture points to Jesus. In some cases it points forward (as in the Old Testament), in some cases backward (as in the New Testament after the Gospels).

[2] Can God use bad methods? Of course he can. But anecdotal stories of how God has used bad methods makes for bad practice. Read Will Metzger, *Tell the Truth* (Downers Grove, Ill.: InterVarsity Press, 1986), especially the first chapter.

Chapter 3. On Your Guard: *Don't Assume the Gospel*

[1] Kevin Roose, *The Unlikely Disciple* (New York: Grand Central Publishing, 2009), p. 152

[2] Ibid., p. 274.

[3] Ibid., p. 313.

[4] This is a variation of a theme put forward by Richard Chinn, IFES General Secretary of Australia.

[5] Roose, *The Unlikely Disciple*, p. 118. My emphasis.

[6] See J. Mack Stiles and Leeann Stiles, *Mack and Leeann's Guide to Short-Term Missions* (Downers Grove, Ill.: InterVarsity Press, 2000).

[7] For example: I live in a place where many are in marriages that were arranged. And I've watched Christian families—mostly from India—arrange marriages with sensitivity and biblical care. It's been a helpful challenge to realize they actually may be closer to the Bible than my culture's understanding of how to get married.

[8] Do not confuse this with ethnicity, which is made by God and in its diversity gives him glory. Critique culture, not ethnicity.

[9] The Student Volunteer Movement (SVM) was a powerful force for world missions in the late nineteenth century that had all but died out fifty years later

because of a growing toleration and eventual espousal of liberal theology.
[10]Roose, *The Unlikely Disciple*, p. 6.

Chapter 4. Does the Message We Share Look Like the Message We Bear? *Living the Implications of the Gospel*

[1]I love short-term mission trips. Read J. Mack Stiles and Leeann Stiles, *Mack and Leeann's Guide to Short-Term Missions* (Downers Grove, Ill.: InterVarsity Press, 2000).

[2]Tim Keller, "The Centrality of the Gospel," pp. 1-2, <www.redeemer2.com/resources/papers/centrality.pdf>.

[3]Jesus himself did this on a number of occasions, cf. Luke 24:27.

[4]Richard Lovelace, referenced in Keller, "Centrality of the Gospel," p. 2, <www.redeemer2.com/resources/papers/centrality.pdf>.

[5]In Philippians 2:12, when Paul says, "Work out your salvation . . ." he means that we should apply the principles of our salvation to our lives.

[6]There are three uses of the law: the first to convict us of our sin, the second to restrain evil in the world and the third to help guide us in ways that please God. But for every discussion about the third use of the law, we should have three conversations about the law of love from Galatians 6:2 and 1 Corinthians 9:21.

[7]Read C. J. Mahaney, *The Cross-Centered Life* (Sisters, Ore.: Multnomah Books, 2002).

[8]Read Rose Marie Miller, *From Fear to Freedom* (Colorado Springs: WaterBrook, 1994) for an excellent treatment of what it means to live as the adopted children of Christ.

[9]D. A. Carson, *Love in Hard Places* (Wheaton, Ill.: Crossway Books, 2002), p. 158.

Chapter 5. Messengers in a Troubled World: *The Gospel and Social Change*

[1]A missionary in Nairobi quoted by Bishop John Taylor in John Stott, *Christian Mission in the Modern World* (Downers Grove, Ill.: InterVarsity Press, 1972), p. 28.

[2]The central city of the Ixil area.

[3]The irony is that in the Ixil area a liberation theology experiment, calling for the oppressed to rise up in rebellion, resulted in murder and poverty.

[4]As G. K. Chesterton pointed out, living in the world is like living on a ship-

wreck: there are many treasures to be found, but they come to us with a sense that things are not right.

[5]Francis A. Schaeffer, *The Mark of the Christian* (Downers Grove, Ill.: InterVarsity Press, 2006, 1970), p. 59.

[6]J. I. Packer, *Evangelism and the Sovereignty of God* (Downers Grove, Ill.: InterVarsity Press, 2008, 1961), pp. 108-9.

[7]A Latin American concept, mostly from Gustavo Gutiérrez, *A Theology of Liberation* (Maryknoll, N.Y.: Orbis Books, 1973, 1988), that combined neo-Marxist thinking with parts of the gospel.

Chapter 6. Waving the Flag: *Understanding True Biblical Conversion*

[1]See Revelation 7:9. Of course there is great irony that it required a Muslim nation to make it happen.

[2]Pastors and elders, don't miss the amazing opportunity for evangelism found in membership interviews.

[3]First Corinthians 5:12 makes it clear churches need to judge the actions of members.

[4]See Luke 24:45. Even here we see it is a work of Jesus' grace to us to understand.

[5]J. I. Packer, *Evangelism and the Sovereignty of God* (Downers Grove, Ill.: Inter-Varsity Press 2008, 1961), p. 57.

[6]Paul E. Little, *How to Give Away Your Faith* (Downers Grove, Ill.: InterVarsity Press, 2008, 2006), p. 119.

[7]Read John Piper, *God Is the Gospel* (Wheaton, Ill.: Crossway Books, 2005).

[8]One reason to quickly disciple new believers is because of their initial excitement about following Christ. We should make sure they are helped before they are swamped by the assault from the world.

[9]Some would respond to this "easy believism" by imposing lots of rules after conversion, but that's approaching it from the back end. By far the biggest problem is on the front end where the gospel is being preached.

[10]There is no better book to understand this than J. I. Packer, *Evangelism and the Sovereignty of God*.

[11]To misunderstand God's action in conversion gives rise to the dangers of pragmatic evangelism that we looked at in chapter one and a tendency to try and take on the role of the Holy Spirit in people's lives.

[12]Anyone with a teenager has immediate understanding on the nature of the miracles contained in that sentence.

Chapter 7. Be Bold: *Slaying the Fear Factor When Sharing Our Faith*

[1]The dialogue in its entirety can be seen at www.youtube.com/watch?v=ciiIqG XwWKo&feature=PlayList&p=2716CDD9C91463D1&index=0>. The DVD is published by GDS, 2009.

[2]Read Edward T. Welch, *When People Are Big and God Is Small* (Phillipsburg, N.J.: P&R Publishing, 1997), on which much of this chapter is based.

[3]Notable among them is D. A. Carson, *A Call to Spiritual Reformation: Priorities from Paul and His Prayers* (Grand Rapids: Baker Academic, 1992).

Chapter 8. Worldly Love and Its Fruits: *Mistaking the World's Love for God's Love*

[1]Not only is it only one of the names, *wadud* is perhaps better translated "affection" from classical Arabic. Sufism would be an exception that proves the rule. Sufis do hold to a loving God, but they tend to be seen as a cult or sect by orthodox Muslims.

[2]A true understanding of Buddhism would see love as a desire and therefore something to be avoided.

[3]Homer Banks, Raymond Jackson and Carl Hampton, "(If Loving You Is Wrong) I Don't Want to Be Right" (Memphis: Stax Records, 1972).

[4]D. A. Carson, *Love in Hard Places* (Wheaton, Ill.: Crossway Books, 2002), p. 18.

[5]D. A. Carson, *The Difficult Doctrine of the Love of God* (Wheaton, Ill.: Crossway Books, 2002). Carson lays the basis for an excellent understanding of five biblical expressions of God's love and how they are different.

[6]Unfortunately this can easily lead to another pop understanding of religion: works righteousness. But we dealt with that in previous chapters.

[7]Michael W. Smith, "Above All" (New York: Sony BMG records, 2001).

[8]Compare also Hebrews 12:2. (But I like most of Michael W. Smith's other songs.)

[9]C. John Miller, *A Faith Worth Sharing* (Phillipsburg, N.J.: P&R Publishing, 1999).

Chapter 9. The Gospel Made Visible: *The Church*

[1]Mark E. Dever, "The Church," in *A Theology for the Church*, ed. Daniel Akin (Nashville: B&H Publishing Group, 2007), p. 782.

[2]This is not the only time Jesus speaks of the world's right to judge. He speaks of Nineveh from Jonah's day rendering judgment on Judgment Day (Matthew 12:41).

[3]Francis A. Schaeffer, The Mark of the Christian (Downers Grove, Ill.: InterVarsity Press, 2006, 1970), p. 43.

[4]Dever, "The Church," p. 767.

[5]Schaeffer, Mark of the Christian, p. 59.

[6]By clear I mean that the message is clear enough so that people who listen are able to repent and believe in Christ.

[7]Mark Dever's book 9 Marks of a Healthy Church (Wheaton, Ill.: Crossway Books, 2000) gives the best treatise on why church membership is biblical. See especially pp. 133-51.

[8]C. J. Mahaney, Humility (Sisters, Ore.: Multnomah, 2005) is a great Christian book in general, and the best book on humility.

[9]An example is our covenant at United Christian Church of Dubai, found at <www.UCCDubai.com>.

[10]Again, Mark Dever's 9 Marks of a Healthy Church builds a strong case for developing church discipline as a way to create a healthy church.

[11]Unforgiveness is the thing Francis Schaeffer points to as one of the greatest hindrances to true community.

Chapter 10. A Manifesto for Healthy Evangelism: *Taking Action*

[1]Actually, the Parks girls have been known to call me M-Dawg behind my back.

[2]Which is merely a summary of the book.

[3]The ESV Study Bible has one of the most succinct and clearest explanations of the "God, Man, Christ, Response" outline I have seen. ESV Study Bible (Wheaton, Ill.: Crossway, 2008), p. 2501.

[4]My book Speaking of Jesus (Downers Grove, Ill.: InterVarsity Press, 1995) has a lot on how to turn conversations to Christ.